Going Pl

How to
network
your way
to
personal success

John Galloway
Anne Gorman

Published By: Allen and Unwin
Social Impacts
Netmap Corporation

Distributed By: Allen and Unwin
Social Impacts

First Edition

Printed by: The Book Printer
Design, typeset and artwork by: Set 'n Type, Sydney
Diagrams and cover art by: Bromide Action, Sydney
Cartoons by Mark Knight, The Australian Financial Review

National Library of Australia
Cataloguing in Publication Data
Galloway, John
Gorman, Anne

Going Places. How to network your way to personal success

Bibliography
ISBN: 0 958 7819 07

For the late Margaret Galloway who inspired the initial ideas and for Wendy, the best networker I know and for Scottie and Phoebe.

– John Galloway

For Alexandra, Austin, Vanessa, Henry and Rebecca who taught me about the most important things in life.

– Anne Gorman

Preface

We all want to get up and go places. In order to achieve this simple objective, we need to meet with others and make the right "connections".

This book is all about connections and how connections come together to make a network, your network. But there are other dimensions.

If you don't actively grow your connections, then there is a grave danger of not growing yourself, of becoming becalmed in a sea of lost opportunity.

There are no mysteries about networking. Anyone can use their connections to work for their success if they change the way they think about their family, business or work connections, their friends and friends of friends. These people make up our most valuable resource, and they want to and expect us to use them to help us on our way. Why? Because some day, any day, they might need that help from us since we too are part of their most treasured resource.

We believe we have demonstrated in this book, that understanding and developing these personal networking skills is absolutely fundamental. You can, should and must, make full use of this basic skill to provide the leverage you need to achieve your goals, no matter what your chosen field of endeavour in business or social life.

This book finally "happened" because of a cross roads network. In 1985, Dr. John Miller introduced the authors to one another since he knew they were both interested in networking.

Most of the people in this book are real people and belong to the two authors' networks. Some didn't mind being identified, others preferred to remain anonymous. Some vignettes are fictional composites of the authors' own experiences or the experience of their friends.

We thank all these people for helping us pass on what we've learned in recent years, namely, that in the information society, you can't do without networks. Networks are the conduits for passing and shaping information, and people are its conductors. And that's why networks have suddenly become so much more important and are causing us to rethink the sanctity and utility of certain concepts such as the long term usefulness of the old boy network.

In particular, we would like to thank John Mappin, Blair Stone and the late Geoff Goddard, who all had a substantial impact on the original draft chapters that John wrote in 1979. Chris Murphy, Mark Hunter, Brian Etheridge, Gillian Feest, Lesley Albertson, Poss and Rob Reynolds, Pat and Tine Brennan, Barbara Mobbs, Barbara Ball, Willie Murphy, Bob Barraket, Mike Hilsden, Larry Berkes, Dr. Thor Yamaguchi and Jim Kelly all contributed in important ways to this endeavour as did Susan Tyrrell, Jill Nash, Matthew Kelly and Mark Knight of the Australian Financial Review, who added the cartoons to complete the book and our editor Dawn Titmus.

We would especially like to acknowledge the work of Christine Johnson who typed most of the original drafts and Debbie McDonald who completed the final manuscript.

We've enjoyed our networked association and the experience of working together. We hope it takes you places you never dreamed of going and that you, like us, enjoy every minute of it.

John Galloway

Anne Gorman

They say he
has some
powerful contacts

CONTENTS

Chapter 1
Networks and Networking
An Introduction to Key Concepts

You are only three phone calls away from the Pope, the President of the United States or from the great new contact who could change your whole life.

In this book we show you how to make those contacts. How to open your life to the opportunities that are just waiting out there for you. Whether you are a clerk in a bank, a young school-leaver, a cleaner, a managing director or a politician, success is yours if you follow the easy steps outlined here and you understand a little about the changing world in which we all live.

Some years ago a well-known sociologist, Stanley Milgram, conducted a series of studies on what he called "the small world". He selected people at random in California and gave them each an envelope. On each envelope was the name and address of a person selected at random on the East Coast of the United States. Each Californian was asked to use his or her acquaintances to get the envelope to the particular destination person on the East Coast in as few network steps as possible. They could not simply mail the envelope to the person; rather, they had to hand deliver or mail the envelope to somebody they knew (and who would know them if so asked) who might be expected to know the destination person or be a step closer to eventually reaching that person.

The upshot of these studies was that Milgram was able to work out how many steps, on average, through acquaintances etcetera, it took to reach any one person (a random destination person on the East Coast) from any other person (a random start person on the West Coast). Before you guess how many steps it would take, recall that 240 million people live in the United States. Because of the huge population, a popular guess is that hundreds of steps might be involved. However, Milgram found that on average any one person can reach any other person via contact through only 5.5 acquaintances, an amazingly low number.

The power of networks is such that a few people who know a few people who know a few people can quickly become a very large number in only a few steps. In the jargon of the advertising industry, the "reach" potential is huge.

Features of the "small world" such as the "reach" potential are being increasingly recognised and acted upon. Networks is now a vogue term. We have peace networks, women's networks, and a host of more local situations such as tenancy networks built around certain issues or problems common to the tenants of an apartment block.

You and Your Network

Joe, Mary, Jane, John, Fred, Tom and you all work together, all grew up together and now spend some of your leisure time in the same group. You are all intimately linked. But if that's all the contacts you have and you have been wondering why your success is limited, then we suggest you read on.

This book is about YOU and about your personal networks, and its purpose is to help you to get the most out of the people you know or will know so that you can go on to be a success. And it is easy because everyone has personal contacts.

By personal network we mean the network of contacts that is closest to you, that is "anchored" upon you. It is more or less an extension of yourself. We do not mean the broader network "out there" that is further away from you, for example, contacts of contacts of contacts of contacts, etcetera. We do not mean some network that you can go and join, that exists independently of you, for example, the women's network or a peace network. At some level of course virtually everybody is indirectly connected to everybody else.

Your immediate personal network comprises all your direct contacts and all the links that may exist between them. For example, take Joe, Mary, Jane, Tom, Fred, John and you. Say your immediate personal network looks like this:

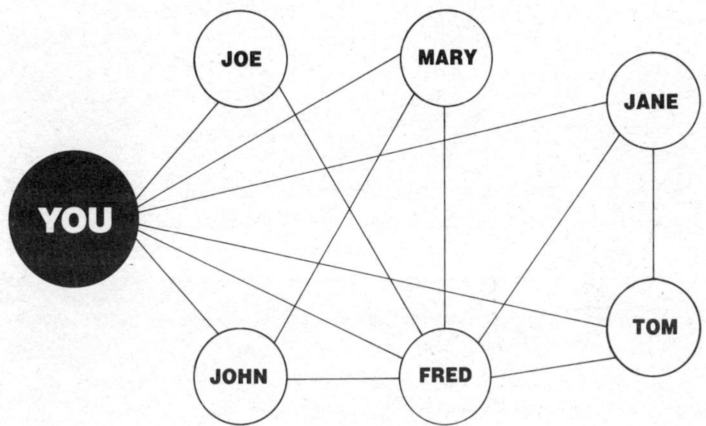

Figure 1.1:
Your personal network

You have links of course to all of your contacts and some of those people are in turn interlinked. Clearly Fred is a key person within this immediate zone of your personal network because Fred has links with all of your contacts. You and Fred *share* many of the same contacts and, therefore, possibly also share many of the same ideas or items of information that happen to be circulating. There is an overlap in communication partners between you and Fred. And the more these communication links are accessed by you and Fred, the more commonality is likely to develop between you.

But for some people their personal network is the extent of their universe. It locks them out of many opportunities – they are limited in what they know and what they can do. In any case whatever the characteristics of your personal network, there is no question that it will have a significant bearing on your chances of success. Therefore, how you develop and manage your personal network is crucial to that success.

Indirect Contacts

Your personal network also includes indirect contacts. In the above example although Fred is obviously a key person, Joe is not so well linked within this immediate zone of your personal network. However, it could be that Joe is well connected to others still who are strategically important from your point of view, (see Figure 1.2). For example, A, B, C or D may be important indirect contacts of yours via Joe.

Or A, B, C and D may be important because they in turn have certain contacts of interest to you – which persons would be still more remote indirect contacts of yours, yet nonetheless part of your extended personal network.

Deborah's bank manager is one of the central office managers in the city branch of a national bank. She first met him after he took over from a previous manager who was promoted to a senior executive position in the bank. Her account was overdrawn and she presented herself with a new business plan – an unknown person, or so she thought, asking for a lot of financial accommodation. Very early on in the meeting the manager asked her if she was related to her sister-in-law, a woman with a different name, living in a different part of the country. It seemed he made the connection because he knew Deborah's maiden name and something of her rural background. He had been her brother's and sister-in-law's bank manager during his long stint in the country. This "connection", tenuous as it was, gave them each a confidence in one another that remained the bond that cemented a very accommodating and happy relationship. They had a link that gave them commonality – but apart from that, the various other contacts, which were enormously diverse, potentially and actually, meant that they were also a potentially valuable resource to each other.

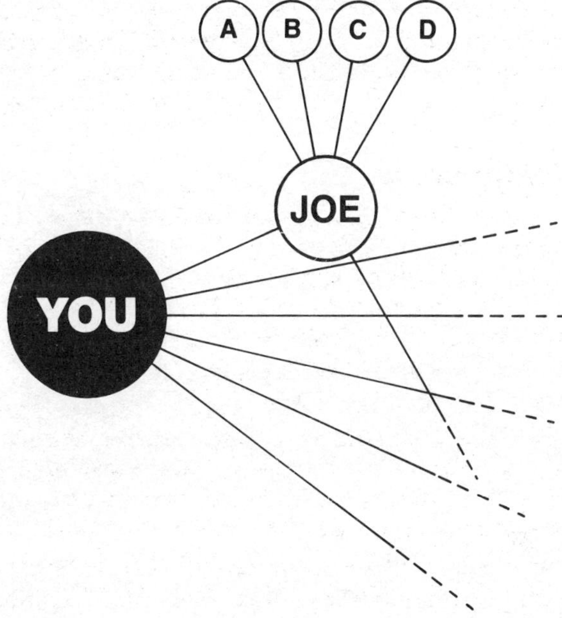

Figure 1.2:
Indirect contacts

This may seem an everyday sort of example and we have used it for precisely that reason. Networking is a skill available to everyone and can be relied on to help in almost every life situation.

Recognising the strengths and weaknesses of your personal networks and managing your networks to advantage, just as you manage other aspects of your life, is a major theme of this book. It is not sufficient merely to set objectives in your mind, think positively and so on. We are all embedded in some sort of network. There is no question that objectives, positive mental attitudes and so forth are all extremely important, but over and above those considerations you must also network your way to the goals that you set for yourself.

Structure and Strategy

Your personal network structure must be in place if you are to be able to achieve your goals, that is, if you are to successfully implement some strategy that you have in mind. The crucial interplay between strategy and structure is well known in management circles (it was first noted by Chandler in *Strategy and Structure*, 1962) – strategy and structure go hand in hand. Just as the structure of an organisation must "fit" the strategy and vice versa, so, too, personal network structures must "fit" the objectives a person has evolved as part of his or her personal strategy. It is just no good having a perfect strategy (carefully set objectives and so on) if the structure into which you are applying the objectives is inappropriate to allow the objectives to be achieved.

For example, say your objective is to join the Wednesday golf group. If you do not know anybody in the Wednesday golf group, perhaps you can think of somebody you do know who in turn knows somebody in the group, or who in turn knows the club president and can arrange an introduction to someone in the group. This is a case of the structure, the network, being adapted to fit the strategy. All too often things happen the other way around; the structure determines the strategy. Somebody's close-knit personal network, for example, often determines what he or she actually knows and sets limits on the sorts of strategies that that person *can* be aware of and develop.

The first thing Neil did when he took up a position as special policy advisor to a State minister, was to identify all the other 27 policy advisors in each ministry. Then he worked out which ministries were of most significance to his job and what he wanted to achieve; who held the power; who had most say over the allocations of the budget; who listened to whom, and so forth. Although he was a newcomer, he soon established links and friendships with all the people who could help most in getting things through the system. He cared little about the formal organisation structure but he developed a strategy and then set about establishing the "real" structure – his own links and friendships, that is, personal networks which would fit closely with his strategic objectives. In fact any strategy just could not work without this network-type structure.

Getting Things Done

Being an innovator, Neil had many new ideas and had been recruited in the hope that he would have some impact on helping his minister review and reform the system that he administered. Neil's minister was constantly amazed at the way Neil managed to achieve agreement over contentious matters before he had to discuss them in Cabinet, but he never asked Neil how he did it.

Although a key and initial link was the support given by David Hill, who was then an economic advisor to the Premier and at the time of writing is the new managing director of the ABC, the links with certain like-minded innovators were also important because they provided the most valuable, reliable and confidential type of information precisely when it was needed so that important opportunities would not be lost.

Because women are often at a severe disadvantage in male societies, like innovators, they, too, have had to develop their networking skills to a high level. The Colonial Sugar Refining Company – which has diversified activities ranging from sugar refining, building materials, mining oil and gas, mineral exploration to agricultural holdings – was one of the first companies in Australia to recruit women to middle and senior management. For more than seven years these women worked in different parts of the organisation, geographically dispersed and isolated from one another.

Two years ago one of the more senior women decided to establish links between women within the organisation. The result is a flourishing network of women supportive of one another and of new recruits. The prospects for women's employment in CSR have vastly improved as a result and the company is pleased because it is ahead of the field in meeting government equal employment opportunity (EEO) objectives. This strategy, once begun, was actively encouraged by management, who also realised it was all part of the need to balance the disadvantage of being a minority group within an organisation historically dominated by male employees.

By contrast the large bank Westpac has more recently recruited women to senior positions. One of its women employees, encouraged by the success at CSR, approached management seeking "permission" to set up a women's network, but was stoutly refused. Management quite understandably were fearful of any activity that would give power to a group that they did not understand or control. The irony is that the Westpac women did not need management "permission" to begin a networking process. Men in Westpac had probably been doing it for years, only they hadn't called it by that name or anything else. CSR's women had started theirs by themselves and only later received management endorsement.

There is another irony. Bob White, the managing director of Westpac is the chairman of the group set up by the Business Council to work with the Federal Government on their affirmative action pilot scheme. Obviously the message had not been sent far enough down the line!

The moral of this story is that networking can proceed without anyone but the people who do it being aware of how they are increasing both their own and others' power within an organisation.

Networks and networking defy formalised behaviour. Their strength lies outside institutional structures, although the process of networking can be used to develop and maintain support for formal structures. The flip side is that networking not only provides the capacity for an organisation to remain responsive, but it also means the organisation must take on a different style. It can no longer operate as a closed shop and people within it will also have to learn to operate differently. Women's networking is part of that much larger development – human networking.

There have been many articles and several very good books on women's networks. *Networks – the great new way for women to get ahead* by Mary Scott Welch, is a most notable example; we do not intend to repeat her excellent and extensive advice here and the lessons apply to everyone. But it is important for women, especially, to know that they do not need to ask "permission" to do what men have been doing for centuries. Women need to be aware that to be a success they have to think about structure and strategy in different ways to the ones their mothers taught them.

Issue Networks

The types of networks referred to by Scott Welch are non-personal, in that they are not anchored on a particular individual. They are generally "issue" networks, for example, women, peace, etcetera, which are of course, much broader than personal networks. They often reflect a series of concerns in a given community or are symptomatic of a broad social movement and, incidentally, of the times in which we live. Let us take an example of the synergy, as well as the essential differences, between personal networks and non-personal or issue networks. For this example we will stay with women's networks, although many other examples are given later in the book.

Susan is the head of a franchised tourist operation and spends a great deal of her time travelling the world. She is a natural networker and maintains contact with both men and women inside and outside her operation and in the tourist trade itself. Because she has learned that new ideas often come from areas outside the trade and because she believes strongly in the women's cause, she also cultivates a kind of sub-network of women whose interests range across many professions – the business and academic worlds and the public service. These women all have one thing in common. They wish to help and support each other and their younger colleagues in the tough job of making it in a male world.

The women's network has frequently provided Susan with valuable inside information that certainly wouldn't have been available from any other source. Because the women share a number of implicit understandings, contact is easy and doors are always opened when Susan needs them. But the network has to be cultivated and kept functioning. Moreover, because the women's network also accesses all spheres of influence, all professions, businesses and ethnic groups, it provides considerable richness of ideas and contacts, a fact that often leaves Susan speechless with delight and repays all the effort she puts into it as well as being a strong motivating factor to continue.

Common Bonds

There is no doubt that people who can find a common bond or area of interest that overrides other interests are in a good position to form networked associations in a wide variety of spheres and to benefit personally from them. Marilyn Ferguson has also pointed out, in the *Aquarian Conspiracy*, the existence of links between people who share a cause or ideal that also transcends class, culture or other factors of geography or birth. In the New Age movement as described by Ferguson, people "discover" each other in a variety of ways and link New Age thinkers into an open, loose coalition. The coalitions often transcend other structural loyalties because they are based on the mutual self-interests of the group and/or on a higher ideal. Common interests, then, often cut across and influence other values and loyalties, as Sharon Lord found during her term at the Pentagon.

Dr Sharon Lord was charged with, among other things, the responsibility for equal employment opportunity and affirmative action. The power of the women's network was never more cogently brought home to her than when she received a phonecall one day from a woman in another part of the military in another State, who refused to name herself. She told Sharon of some important policy changes being mooted at the Pentagon, which were to have serious repercussions on her budget and, indeed, the whole EEO policy. Sharon's informant, whose identity she never discovered, told her that the plan was to inform her of changes as part of a broader restructure, when it would be too late to change the policy. Needless to say, Sharon was able to take immediate action and confront the key Pentagon power-brokers involved, who were astounded that she knew of their plans. The plans were ultimately changed. The power-brokers had backed off.

No doubt the military accommodates many similar networks and always has. People who fought together in a campaign have a common bond, the group who met through officer training together, marines, commandos etc. etc. So a sex related network is nothing new.

Common Cause

In Part II we discuss in greater depth the emergence of issue networks of the kind described by Ferguson and many others. These are part of a uniquely modern phenomenon. People who have a common interest can now communicate with one another with relative ease. They are better educated in this century than in the last; they can read about new ideas; they can swap experiences; they can take action simultaneously. They are a force to be reckoned with.

Returning to Susan. She travels a great deal and thus she is able to keep in touch with key members of the network wherever she goes just by dropping selected people a note occasionally or calling them if she's travelling through their city. She never misses an opportunity to help various members when asked or to make time when they call her. She has learned two major lessons: the first is that some people are key members of the network and give access to many other members, so by keeping in touch with them she automatically has access to many others; the second is that reciprocity is the key.

Reciprocity is not keeping score. It is doing what you have to do or are asked to do at the time, knowing that it doesn't work on a one-for-one basis. The help and assistance is shared around the network, and in the end you get more than you give and more often than not the opportunities this brings far exceed the original time and energy invested.

In Susan's case she uses the network to access hard-to-get, informal "underground" information about the background to a business deal or the honesty of a new business associate. Once or twice that information has saved her from wasting excessive sums of money or employing the wrong person and she has learned to trust her network implicitly. Mostly Susan manages to discover everything she needs to know in three phonecalls. If she has to go further than that she thinks again about her starting point. She knows without the benefit of having read Milgram that it doesn't take much to make the right contacts.

However, any number of people might have been involved in helping Susan gain the information that she needs. Sometimes others make calls and call her back – they might speak to several other people, men and women. They might arrange an introductory lunch, or tell her someone else is on the same trail, so she might need to link up with them or alternatively be aware of her competitors and how and with whom they are negotiating.

Common Characteristics

Networks of all sorts, whether anchored on an individual or based around a series of issues, have certain characteristics in common.

The idea of sharing is central – that people get together and share experiences, ideas and information to mutual advantage. "One up, one down" (↑ ↓) relationships are minimal, and hence there is little bureaucracy and asymmetry is unimportant. Everybody relates to everybody else or they can do so in theory; hence there are many symmetrical relationships (⇆). Communication occurs *with* somebody, not to them, and all of this occurs because of underlying assumptions about the importance of reciprocity of behaviour and actions performed that are mutually beneficial.

Sharing, mutuality, commonality, etcetera? So What?

Networks give people feelings of participation in voluntaristic, less threatening, less committed, less "one up, one down" ways than in a regular organisation or association. There is, therefore, an air of informality, and informal relationships most often underpin what actually goes on. Different expectations guide what happens, and the unwritten rules can be extremely powerful and highly motivating.

This book is not about networking in the sense of community issue networks or broader social movement networks. However, the above examples clearly illustrate the spin-offs and connections between these types of networks and personal networks. You can join the broader networks, of course, as distinct from personal networks that you already belong to, that are, in effect, very much a part of you, an extension of you.

Regardless of your participation in issue networks, whether you are a man or a woman, you will be embedded in various personal networks as the anchor point of those connections. And, therefore, you have considerable control over those sets of relationships and fairly immediate potential impact upon them. You can most readily lever your personal network to advantage and "grow" it over time to match your objectives. This you cannot do with larger issue networks. This is a crucial distinction – *you* can control your own personal networks. In fact, you have to, to succeed.

In the next chapter we discuss how you can start to think of yourself as the centre of an ever expanding network, whether you are linked to a group that shares the same ideals as you do or not.

Checklist

Chapter 1

- The nature of your personal network has a significant bearing on your chances of success.
- Recognising and managing your personal network is crucial for success.
- Strategy and structure go hand in hand. They must fit the personal objectives you set yourself.
- Networks and networking are a major resource and provide freedom to succeed.
- You do not need permission to network – go ahead make your personal network work for you.
- Personal networks are different from issue networks. Personal networks you can directly control, in fact, you must if you are to succeed.
- Issue networks, however, can provide a powerful sense of commonality and implicit understandings between people when making connections.
- Networked affiliations are less formal than regular organisational membership.
- You are embedded in various personal networks and you are the anchor point for those networks.
- You can grow your personal networks over time to match your objectives.

Chapter 2

Nobody can do Anything Important Alone

Extending Yourself Through and With Others: "You" = You and Your Personal Network

No person is an island – what counts is who you know and why this counts is who they know that you don't. Thus if you have developed skills and achieved objectives that have led to success, it is almost certain that the journey has not been undertaken independently of others. The self is simply not big enough to achieve significant success without their help. We are social beings and the better we understand this and use it to advantage the more successful we will become.

Other people, from the viewpoint of the self, serve as a major resource for extensions of the self. Consciously or not, we are all networkers. We network our way along through life with greater and lesser degrees of success. Many of us are, in fact, trapped by our networks because we have not taken a long, hard look at them. If we look fairly carefully at who we are connected to and, in turn, who they are connected to, it is possible to see the degree to which we have become a prisoner of our own networks. Then by giving emphasis to particular sorts of contacts we can see opportunities that will have a liberating effect.

This may seem coldly calculating, but since we are all networkers anyway and our contacts are a major resource to each one of us, we might as well get on with it and do it properly. Successful individuals and successful organisations cannot afford to tolerate inefficient usage of these incredibly valuable resources. For that is what they are – the contacts that we have and that we have worked so hard to develop over the years are a major resource, a resource that we should nurture and manage as carefully as any other major resource.

George is an up-and-coming administrator who uses his networking skills to accelerate his mobility. If he is going to a conference he either gets himself on the list of speakers or, at an appropriate and key moment, introduces himself from the floor and asks a penetrating and interesting question. It works every time, he says, and many of the people at the conference with the same interests as he has manage to introduce themselves later and give him their card.

Listening

No matter how insignificant the person might appear to be, George always listens intently to their opinion even if they disagree and generally drops them a short line on his return home. This way he has developed a large number of admirers and a network of influence, power and business associates unavailable to many of his colleagues (who still wonder how he does it), as well as some trusted and valuable close friends.

The technique has worked very well for him on two occasions when he has moved to new jobs. Waiting carefully until he understands the culture of his new workplace and choosing his moment and the right occasion, he asks a question aimed at building a network of support for his ideas. Often this is done well after his arrival and only after he has assessed in what form this new culture will accept the new idea and him along with it. George has learned many lessons and the first is to wait, watch and read with accuracy the culture, mood, power or whatever you like to call it of the group and individuals within it.

He has discovered, for example, that a question that contains within it room for others, displays an openness for discussion. This does not jeopardise his intellectual integrity but it does invite dialogue and, unlike a definitive statement that

Connections : How it works

closes the debate, draws people to him for an interchange. It is on the basis of such subtleties that networked resources are built and then managed.

Taking Stock of Our Contacts

Whatever the motives, everyone of us can manage our personal networks better and, therefore, make a significant difference toward achieving our goals – if we take stock of our contacts carefully and make personal network decisions that will improve our positions. This advice is intended to be of benefit to virtually everyone, for everyone has personal networks. However, it is especially directed to people in two situations:

1. If you have read many of the "how to succeed" books and think there is still room for improvement – you could be even more successful – you are urged to read on.
2. If you are, or feel, relatively powerless in your current circumstances – whether the background to your powerlessness stems from minority group membership or otherwise – then you, too, are urged to read on.

What sorts of benefits might be expected from this advice? In the case of readers of "success" genre books, and attendees at different courses, no doubt you have filled your mind with positive thoughts and self-images in order to succeed. You know where you are going in life in a deliberate and positive manner. But each of us is a social being; it is not enough to be positive in outlook but yet alone, independent of others. It is crucial to think positively but you must also network your way to success. And before you can say that you've established the right personal networks and managed them appropriately, you need to take stock of your current network patterns and appraise them in relation to your objectives. Will your personal network be a hindrance or a help?

If you feel you haven't got much power, you need to take similar steps. Only here it will be helpful to recognise that there is a steadily growing worldwide movement toward the establishment of networks to achieve goals at grassroots level called the self-help movement or "issue networks", which we have referred to in Chapter 1. The skills to help you break out of power defined situations can become much better developed by taking stock of your current patterns of relationships and marrying them with a set of objectives that you decide upon (see Chapter 8, "Achieving Your Personal Objectives").

You *must* become well connected if you are to succeed. But what does "well connected" mean? What does a personal network mean? Networks are simply patterns of relationships that exist between people. People interact with each other frequently or importantly, or have some other sorts of criteria for relationships, for example friendship, significant work contacts, professional contacts, sporting, recreation, travelling companions. Each of us has relationships in these and similar areas. Our own personal networks are those that are anchored upon ourselves, for example, you, plus all of your close friends, plus all of the outer connections between them.

Disadvantage Turned to Opportunity

When Anne was working at the public service she noticed many of the people who worked there lived in the mountains or on the coast and travelled as much as two hours a day each way to and from work. One of her staff, we will call him Ian, was one such person. He often arrived at work with useful information that he didn't have the night before. Anne was always puzzled by that until she discovered that the train to Gosford offered untold opportunities for networking and information-sharing. Many of the people who travelled with Ian did not use this opportunity for their own benefit or the benefit of their work. They teamed up every morning with the same group, often from the one department, and played cards or gossiped and read their papers. But Ian noticed that the train carried people from almost every government department and from various companies as well. Because he belonged to two sporting clubs and to a school parents' group in

Gosford, he already knew something about many of the people on the train from these associations and he asked these people to introduce him to others.

Once Ian came to work with a vital piece of information, dropped casually by one of his fellow travellers. The Premier's Department was considering Anne's submission for extra funding for a major new project that had involved two years' work by a team of researchers. Because the officer she had briefed in Premier's had been taken ill, it had been given to another unsympathetic officer to vet before going to Cabinet. Ian had gathered other information that would be useful in the longer term as well. The Premier's Department was being restructured – a number of people were being moved. This provided Anne with an immediate strategy. She recalled the submission, suggesting that new budget information had come to hand. She thus regained the initiative. When the restructure was over, she sent the submission back to the same section but only after establishing that the friendly officer had returned from sick leave and had been thoroughly rebriefed.

Ian used his networks on the train effectively in all sorts of other ways. He met people who widened his horizons and who offered him other opportunities. His capacity to use information to enhance his current boss's position in the way described, together with his energy and ability, had to be rewarded everywhere he went. He quickly moved through the ranks to a senior position, then into another department, and has now been headhunted into the private sector at double his previous salary. Some people felt that travelling long distances to work was a severe disadvantage and there is no doubt it can be. Ian turned a disadvantage into an opportunity, and through his journeys backwards and forwards built universally broad networks, was rewarded with extraordinarily useful information and, ultimately, with success.

The personal networks in which each of us is embedded act either (and sometimes in both ways) to constrain or liberate us. If we can develop the right contacts at the right time we can move across to other fields of endeavour, friendship or opportunity. Many goals we set can only be realised if we are linked with others who can sanction or facilitate the steps necessary to achieving those goals or objectives.

To the Top

Bev Dyke discovered this wisdom early in her work career. She is now a young chief executive of Mojo Corporate, the highly successful public relations adjunct to one of the most creative advertising agencies in Australia.

The only child of a retiring woman – who lost her husband soon after Bev's birth and who had to work as a clerk to keep both Bev and her ageing parents – Bev has had to make it to the top without the advantages of money, or those wealthy and powerful family contacts that some successful people take for granted. At the age of 17 Bev presented herself, scrubbed and well groomed, for two job interviews carrying typing qualifications under her arm and not much else. The two jobs she had to choose from were the typist secretary for a young corporate takeover group that was connected to the Australia Party – a party with high ideals, businessman Gordon Barton's backing, a few idealistic optimists and that's all; or a job with IBM.

Her interview with Barton's outfit was scheduled first. Bev saw only the administrative chaos they were in and, perceiving it as ineptitude, mentally turned down this job offer on the spot. The second interview with IBM seemed safer and more promising and she walked ten blocks to that interview with higher hopes. Anyone who saw the film *Nine to Five* or has ever worked in a large open-plan office of secretaries might picture the rows and rows of desks and typewriters that confronted Bev at IBM. She ran the ten blocks back to the Barton operation, hoping that the job there had not gone – a decision that was to open up the many new and challenging contacts and opportunities to which she now attributes her success.

Imagine the environment and the effect of those new contacts on a young, intelligent, impressionable girl. The Barton organisation and the Australia Party had gathered together a group of bright graduates who worked feverishly from a sense of a new vision for Australia. With no chance of electoral success for years, they saw their role as catalysts or change agents. The impressionable young Bev caught their feverish idealism while listening intently to their intellectual discussions. She studied part-time for a university degree, and when the party moved its headquarters to Melbourne, she was offered a job as a producer for a political commentator for one of the major Sydney radio stations. Later she was offered an opportunity to be a shareholder director in a public relations firm, which was built up to become a thriving business. Her recent joint venture with Mojo MDA has rocketed her to prominence and of course at every turn her network has grown quite extensively.

Bev's success can largely be attributed to hard work, reliability, energy, intelligence, imagination, a capacity to take risks – and her extensive networks. She never forgets her old friends nor does she forget those people to whom she owes so much of her early learning – most of whom have themselves moved on to more successful careers in other spheres. These have opened, in turn, wider opportunities both for themselves and for their new and old network of friends and colleagues.

However, networks can constrain and prevent the attainment of goals because of close-knitted patterns of contacts that circulate localised and provincial views, virtually causing the entrapment of the individual within his or her own personal network. We discuss this aspect further in Chapter 7 ("Locked into Z-Ville, Locked Out at Y-Ville") and Chapter 10 ("The Old Boy Network").

Success stories of businesspeople are very much the flavour of the month in Australia today. It is remarkable how many of these successful people have stepped out of an old country into a new, and seemed not to have been constrained by either the old or the new. Robert Holmes à Court, Peter Abeles, Alan Bond and Larry Adler are all good examples of this new genre. Likewise, John Elliott does not belong to the Melbourne establishment, neither does Bob Ansett, the son of Reg, who made good in spite of rather than because of his father.

It was this quality to think independently of the crowd, to escape from the constraints of the small pond that allowed Peter Abeles to make strong connections to the Labor government in New South Wales when it unexpectedly came to power in 1976. Other more conservative businesspeople were held back by their allegiances to the conservative parties. They went looking, rather belatedly, for friends at court a few years later, but much opportunity had by then been lost.

Extensions of Self

Each of these successful people extended themselves through and with others and did so without looking over their shoulders at the constraints that their peers might have put on them if they had allowed that to happen.

In a very real sense, then, we can extend ourselves through and with others. The chauffeur becomes interesting because he is connected with the people he chauffeurs. The Queen's aide-de-camp is closely connected with the Queen, and therefore a meeting with the aide-de-camp gives one a feeling of psychological proximity to the Queen. One is only one step removed from the Queen in her personal network. Information – and power-brokers position themselves to be close in their personal networks to many important persons. Talking with them is almost like talking with the particular important people. The power-broker is a "representative" of the people to whom he or she is allegedly connected. Take away the connections and the power-broker falls over. They are virtually a product of their own network with their personality reflecting their network. The network defines them – it elaborates their personality and simultaneously puts constraints on who they can be and what they can do.

Just as the power-broker gets defined in a role position for better or for worse, according to his or her contacts, so do you and I. When I meet you, from my point of view you are a kind of representative of all of those other people with whom you are in contact or who I think you have connections to. I don't just meet some sort of "inner" you, the individualistic person whom the "success" books address in terms of setting goals and so forth, I also meet and am far more interested in a sort of social or "extended" you – that is, you plus (indirectly) all of your contacts.

As we said at the beginning, looked at another way, no person is an island. What counts often is who you know and *why* this counts is who they know (and who knows what) that you don't. Your contacts are obviously important in and of themselves, but they are also important because they in turn have contacts who can make or break *your* chances of success. If you don't even have access to them you often can't even get to the starting blocks.

This book is about taking stock of and capitalising upon your extended self. For it is your extended self (you plus your personal network) that gives you the capability to succeed through and with others, and this you need to focus on as well as your inner self that concerns personal goals, ambitions and so on.

Checklist

Chapter 2

- Our friends and connections are our greatest resource. It is not possible to achieve important things independently.
- Networks can allow us to extend ourselves.
- Openness invites dialogue.
- Your personal networks need to be married with the objectives you set for yourself.
- Objectives without the means to achieve them have a poor chance of being met.
- Make the most of unexpected opportunities. Not all networking is planned and directed.
- The more contacts you have, the greater your chances of those unexpected opportunities occurring.
- Become aware of the way you think. Does your thinking lock you into or out of extended opportunities?
- Close-knit networks define us and our behaviour. They can constrain our thinking, our identity and our opportunities.

Chapter 3

What They Tell You is Only Half the Story

You Must Set Your Goals but Also Network Your Way to Success: "Success" = Positive Attitudes and Personal Networks

What do Matthew, Mark, Luke and John, Norman Vincent Peale, Dale Carnegie, Robert Ringer, Maxwell Maltz and Napoleon Hill have in common? All are authors. Yes – what else? All are authors of "success" books, books that show the reader how to grab hold of that elusive thing called success – the forward-looking, positively oriented variety that can be attained only by shaking loose old habits of mind and developing new approaches to point the way.

The setting of objectives, goals and so forth is absolutely fundamental and unchallenged as the basic ingredient to success. All the "success" books say so and all can't be wrong. Or can they?

There's More to it Than "Fixing up One's Head"

In our view these authors are largely correct – but it is a matter of not only, but also... Not only do you need a positive mental attitude, not only do you need a favourable self image, and not only do you need to plan your life by the setting of objectives, but also you must take account of your personal networks so that you *can* achieve success. The individual and mental ingredients to success are crucial. Yet the chances are that you or somebody you know has read most of the "success" genre books, become positive of mind, developed improved self-images and so on, and although these have helped, you or the other person *still* has not really succeeded.

Picture Carmen, a housewife who wanted to get out and do something interesting with her life in addition to raising three glorious children. She started with the "success" books – bought motivational tapes, thought oh so positively, and nothing changed. Why was her life not changing dramatically as the "success" books promised it would?

What Carmen did not realise until later was that, important as the process of fixing up one's head is, this is but part of the equation. It is also necessary to see to it that you have the right connections that can allow your objectives to be reached. Or else your connections will not only mean missed opportunities, they will actually pin you down in the same (supportive and therefore comfortable) situation forever and a day.

Carmen finally built links with a group of other women whose purpose was to help housewives through the transition period between being a housewife and obtaining outside paid work. Through that network she took a highly recommended short training course and was recruited by the course organisers into a part-time job near her home. With the encouragement of the women's network, she has gone on to further studies and her network grows in proportion to her increasing success. She is just about to start her own business with first customers guaranteed by an enthusiastic network.

As Carmen's story illustrates, we are not advocating a wholesale realignment of ties and allegiances that have taken many years to accumulate. Rather, it is suggested that – as a result of reading this book – you may need to prune your personal networks or extend them further in certain directions. Before these steps can be taken however, you need to make an inventory of what your networks are like so that appropriate adjustments can be made. But before we launch into these topics, let's do a quick round-up of the arguments put forward in some of the best-selling "success" books. Firstly, we will look at what might be called "individualistic" approaches; secondly "one-on-one" relationships, and thirdly, a "networker's" approach.

Successful "Success" Books

One of the most successful "success" books has been Norman Vincent Peale's *The Power of Positive Thinking*. It has sold millions of copies and appealed to many because of its practical approach to everyday problems – think positively, refuse to accept thoughts of defeat, believe fully in yourself, etcetera – along with a strengthened sense of optimism through Christian faith.

Many of these points are reiterated or restated in various ways by other notable writers. These include Napoleon Hill – his *Think and Grow Rich* expands the thinking positively approach into many examples and specific pointers for achieving success. Sales books of all sorts have picked up the Dale Carnegie *How to Win Friends and Influence People* story, with admixtures from Peale, Hill and others, to emphasise enthusiasm, drive and the will to succeed that will be harnessed through positive goal-seeking approaches, which result in increased sales and improved income.

The "good news" is usually accepted in terms of feelings of rebirth, a born-again release from the entrapments of habitual patterns of thought. Old thoughts are replaced by positive meanings, goals, and purposes to life and afterlife. Success becomes easier as one works away at developing a liberating and positive self-image – in fact, a new image in Christ's image.

Maxwell Maltz in *Psychocybernetics* suggests that the mind is like a computer. You can let your mind evoke weak and negative self-images, or else you can program it, much as you would a computer, with positive thoughts and positive self-images. Things *will* happen and you *will* succeed. The setting of goals and objectives, the adopting of a positive mental attitude and self-image, the planning and commitment that necessarily go into a successful venture, the importance of visualisation, dreams and so forth – all of these are various hooks or signposts that the "success" genre books describe extremely well.

Game Plans

Books that go beyond the individualistic approach include Robert Ringer's *Winning Through Intimidation*. Ringer argues that success is achieved not only from holding the right attitudes, but also from carefully devised game plans to ensure that efforts will lead to the attainment of goals. That is, implementation phases in the success venture are given emphasis, particularly in terms of how interaction occurs with others. Basically Ringer's emphasis is on buyer/seller relationships illustrated in the context of large-scale real-estate negotiations.

Although this is certainly a step in the right direction – away from a focus solely on individualistic attitudes – Ringer falls short of a full recognition of personal networks and their role in facilitating or impeding the attainment of goals. Ringer's game plans seem to centre on protection against destroyed or dented self-images that can detract from one's movement along a path toward success. Important as this is, it is still not a positive approach toward networking one's way to success. According to Ringer, during contact with others, game plans can be put into operation rather like safety shields that prevent or minimise self-images being shattered. Unless you are equipped to handle these experiences the filling of the mind with positive thoughts will not be sufficient in and of itself. Hence to Ringer success is not only a function of individual and mental attributes. The way one interacts with others is also important. There is a shift toward understanding one-on-one relationships that are developed and managed, specifically buyer/seller relationships. We shall look at this question of one-on-one relationships shortly.

Management By Objectives

It is hardly surprising that many "success" books have been written mainly for managers and sales staff with the purpose of teaching them to think positively, develop self-confidence and so on. This was especially the case in the 1970s when managers were also encouraged to set short-term objectives and long-term goals, and to stretch themselves usually via seminar commitments toward the achievement of high levels of performance and satisfaction. Management by objectives (MBO) programs were instituted throughout large and small organisations. Managers and their subordinates would carefully appraise their strengths and weaknesses, and together decide what were achievable targets. These would be reviewed from time to time as would the objective-setting processes themselves.

This forward-looking, positively oriented and goal-seeking emphasis represented a significant step in the right direction. The trouble was that in some cases people became so fastidious in setting their objectives that they forgot to actually do things. Planning, planning, planning, but little in the way of action – a sure recipe for not succeeding. Or else the setting of objectives became a mechanical set of procedures followed so closely that they constrained managers from taking entrepreneurial and innovative action to get things done, or even to be able to see that things needed to be done. If things didn't fit the plan, too bad. The customer with the broken axle didn't necessarily agree.

We doubt very much, for example, if Jenny, our super salesperson described in Chapter 9 ("Network Liberation in the Information Society"), thought very much about management by objectives. But she did instinctively know that people respond to being cared about and they became loyal customers when they got extraordinarily good service.

The turning of the tide against the more mechanistic and unthinking versions of MBO led to some interesting variations. Programs started to include more emphasis on interpersonal relationships within the processes of setting goals.

Still later developments included reference not just to relationships, but to whole patterns of relationships of networks that were necessary to bring about change. Rosabeth Moss Kanter's book *The Change Masters*, for example, outlines a number of ways in which innovative people get things done in organisations. Her research leads her to the conclusion that the most successful innovators are those who have moved around the organisation from section to section and have built links and alliances over time in a number of places. Our story is running ahead of itself, but to illustrate that networking is fundamental to achieving management by objectives, consider this case of a colleague.

Bruce is a marketing executive. His objective is to beat the opposition to the market with a new product. To do so, he needs to hit the market six months ahead of his competitors. He might pull it off, he reckons, if the rest of the marketing people make it a priority, if he can gain agreement between the workers and the union reps to work about 40 hours overtime and if there are no stoppages, if the distribution end is freed up in time and if the production department delivers as they think they can. He has contacts in each of these areas and he spends as much time networking them into a cohesive group so they work together as a team as he does on the technicalities. And the celebration at the end will include everyone.

One-On-One Relationships

A second emphasis on approaches to success, beyond the individualistic approach, has been a focus on the nature of relationships between individuals. And of course interpersonal relationships are the building blocks of networks. However, the relationships emphasis has been very much a one-on-one affair – for example supervisor/subordinate; parent/child; doctor/patient; mother/daughter; etcetera – rather than any suggestion of real concern as to how various relationships between many people come together to form a pattern or network.

Giving primacy to relationships takes things beyond the individual in that an individual's actions are assumed to be understood in terms of his or her relationships with others. The individual cannot be understood in isolation. The behaviours and emotions that he or she exhibits are conditioned through relationships with others, and it is therefore impossible to act completely individually. One can only act in relation to the presence or absence of others, and the repertoire of expectations and so on that are held by others. Action and reaction flow into one another and the relationship itself takes on a quality that is over and above the separate actions of the two participating individuals. Relationships might be variously described as warm, friendly, close, broad, important, reliable, about this and not that, face to face, via telephone, formal, informal, difficult, business like and so on.

For example, transactional analysis (see Eric Berne's *Games People Play* and *What Do You Say After You Say Hello?*) allows an individual's behavior to be better understood by focusing upon the relationship that he or she develops with another person (for example, husband and wife, teacher and student, boss and subordinate, and so on). Transactions consist of a stimulus (S) and a response (R) between two people, and both people can be in one of three ego states, such that they act like a parent, an adult, or a child. If one of the persons, for example, asks "How much is three times five?" and the other responds "I hate maths!", this is represented diagrammatically by the Figure 3.1.

But if the same question elicits a response of "15", then this is represented diagrammatically by the figure on the next page. Where relationships are "crossed", as in the figure on the left, rather than "complementary", as in the figure on the right, there are potential problems. In this sense, an individual's behaviour can be better understood by reference to that person's one-on-one relationships.

James had trouble understanding the recurring behaviour of Elspeth, one of his most valued staff members. She always

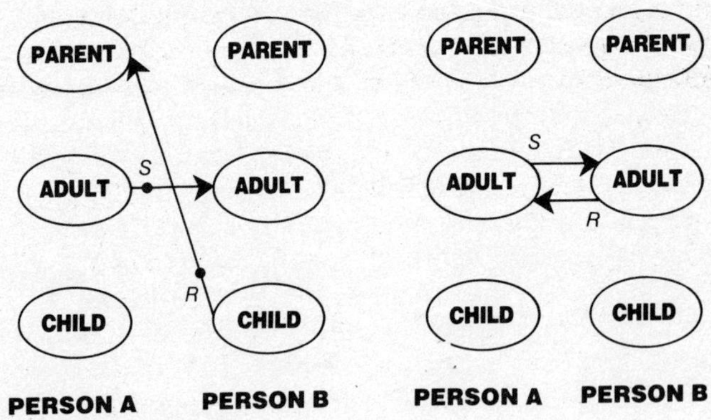

S:Stimulus R:Response

Figure 3.1
Example of "crossed" and "complementary" relationships.

presented him with a *fait accompli* at the last minute when it was too late to change arrangements. Finally he had it out with her, and later sought advice from a psychologist on the staff who was able to explain the dynamics of Elspeth's behaviour.

Elspeth had always managed to get what she wanted but never through open negotiation. The pattern began from early childhood, with a father who always said no when approached directly. The learned behaviour was reinforced in two marriages, both of which ended in divorce. She pursued this pattern of "getting her own way" until her boss finally confronted the situation and then the real meaning behind the way in which she related to him (he the parent authority figure, she the determined, devious, recalcitrant child) came as a revelation to her. Her pattern of behaviour had also succeeded in locking her into relationships with others that reinforced her problem, and even the diagnosis offered no real and immediate escape without a wider perspective and motivation for change.

Success-oriented books that stress the relationships approach include Thomas Harris' *I'm OK, You're OK,* William

Anthony's *Managing Your Boss*, Blanchard and Johnson's *One Minute Manager*, and Thomas Gordon's stable of books, which include *Parent Effectiveness Training* (parent/child relationships), *Leadership Effectiveness Training* (boss/subordinate relationships), and *Teacher Effectiveness Training* (teacher/student relationships).

Networks

A third emphasis on approaches to success has recently evolved. This is a focus on networks. Obviously individuals are fundamental to networks, individuals are very much enmeshed in them, and one-on-one relationships are crucial for they are the building blocks of networks. A network is a set of individuals with relationships between them. So a network emphasis entails both individualistic concerns about thinking positively and setting goals and objectives and so on, as well as a one-on-one relationships emphasis. However, it goes a step further to include many one-on-one relationships. It is the interlocking of these one-on-ones, that is, the interrelationships, that allow us to say something about an individual and his or her location in a network and the extent to which he or she is strategically positioned, for example, well connected or poorly connected.

One of Elspeth's problems was that she sought only those people who reinforced her anti-authority behaviour. Her rebelliousness was charming and funny in its own way, as was her independent spirit; however she found it hard to work in a team. In network terms there was no way she could conceive of an alternative role, of alternative behaviour. Her one-on-one relationships all tended to be of a similar type, with Elspeth in the child role and each of the other persons in the parent role.

The reinforcing nature of this situation is apparent. She was locked into viewing herself and being expected by others with whom she had developed recurring relationships to be rebellious and to be anti-authority. The difficult relationship with James, although important, was but one link in a network that enmeshed her in that type of behaviour. Elspeth needed to grow up and into wider spheres of influence and association. She could drive her boss slowly mad as she had done others, and she could leave a trail of destruction behind her and never have to really deal with any of it until James provided the day of reckoning. She needed to face the truth that her choice of the members of her network constantly reinforced this situation.

In management circles, one of the most successful books ever written, Tom Peter's and Robert Waterman's *In Search of Excellence*, argues that innovation in organisations occurs largely through informal contacts, through the networks that people themselves evolve. Innovation occurs less often through a conscious and formally managed process and far more often through cooperative teamwork – those relationships that people forge themselves – beyond the formal reporting lines. People do build networks of relationships, and the basis for excellence cannot be just individualistic.

Other widely acclaimed management books that support the idea of networks as a basis for success in organisations include Rosabeth Moss Kanter's *The Change Masters*, mentioned earlier, and John Kotter's *The General Managers*. Another two books that advocate recognition of the importance of networks are John Naisbitt's *Megatrends* and Marilyn Ferguson's *The Aquarian Conspiracy*.

Positive Networking

In summary, if things don't work properly and you have read all the "success" books, you might well conclude that you don't have a sufficiently positive attitude – you are not properly committed to your goals, it's your fault, you are to blame for not "fixing your head up" properly. This is an individual problem that can be overcome by a more disciplined approach to the task at hand, more careful setting of objectives and the forging of a positive mind-set, and considerably more effort on your part.

We subscribe strongly to the individualistic approaches such as those that stress the importance of positive thinking and individual effort. These are basic ingredients to achieving success. But if you have read all the success books and still not fully succeeded, then you need to add the power of positive networking to your powers of positive thinking. Some people will be highly successful from thinking positively because they happen to be good networkers. But for many of us thinking positively, as crucial as it is, is not sufficient in itself. As Carmen found, once we take stock of and manage our networks of relationships with others so that we are well connected where it counts, then we can achieve our objectives. Positive thinking and positive networking go hand in hand down the road to success.

Checklist

Chapter 3

- Fixing your head up – developing positive attitudes, setting goals and so on – is only half the story. As important as these aspects of success are you must also network your way to success.
- We rely as much on our contact with many others as we do on individual objectives or positive attitudes, or on one-to-one individualistic relationships.
- Networking is action-oriented – it is about interpersonal relationships and patterns of those relationships.
- Don't get trapped into believing simplistic mechanistic prescriptions that ignore your personal networks; properly managed, your personal networks can make the difference between succeeding and failing.

Chapter 4
Big Fish in Small Ponds
Taking Stock of Who You Are Connected To and Who They Are Connected To

Networks can stifle your chances of success or else greatly increase them. You will not really know until you see what your network looks like. In this chapter we are going to ask you to become actively involved in mapping your own networks. The previous chapter outlined some of the reasons why making the right connections was crucial to success and why new chances have been opened to people in everyday situations. This is the why of networking. This chapter addresses the how of that same process. People are often locked in because they don't realise they are locked in or, if they do realise, they don't know how to change the situation. So in order to find out if this applies to you, the first thing to do is to take stock of who you are connected to and who they are connected to.

Your Relationships

You no doubt have many different types of links with others (friendship, business, recreation, etcetera). For this initial inventory of your personal networks, we want you to focus on any type of relationship that comes to mind as meaningful to you. Perhaps you can visualise the people and the generalised sorts of networks that they belong to.

For example, think of your seven* most frequent, most important or most reliable contacts. This could be in a social, professional or work context. If in a social context, and if you have a regular partner, you might want to think of relationships between couples whom both of you know rather than focussing upon individuals. You might specify the context further if appropriate, for example who are your most frequent and/or important contacts in different areas: fishing, golfing or dining out; finance, production or marketing; shopping, vacations or fashion, etcetera.

Once you have in mind a definition of what *you* mean by a relationship or a link, write the names or initials of each person in the circles below (Figure 4.1):

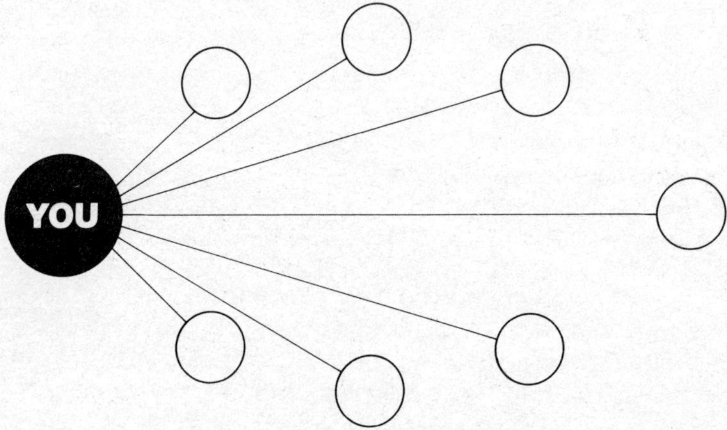

Figure 4.1
Diagram for pencilling in your personal network.

---

* *Seven direct contacts is a number that seems to suit many people. However if this number is limiting you might want to use a blank piece of paper instead of Figure 4.1 and increase the number of people shown. Alternatively, if seven is too many you might want to ignore, say, the lower portion in Figure 4.1.*

You've got to feel sorry for the poor little fella... existing in a small bowl, unaware of what's going on in the big world outside....
TIME CLOCK
KNIGHT

Now think carefully about the relationships (same definition) between all of your direct contacts, that is, the people whom you have said you are directly connected to. Draw in the lines to indicate these cross-connections where they exist, that is between all of the people with whom you are directly connected.

Two Patterns

Either of two sorts of patterns of relationships will result (Figures 4.2 and 4.3).

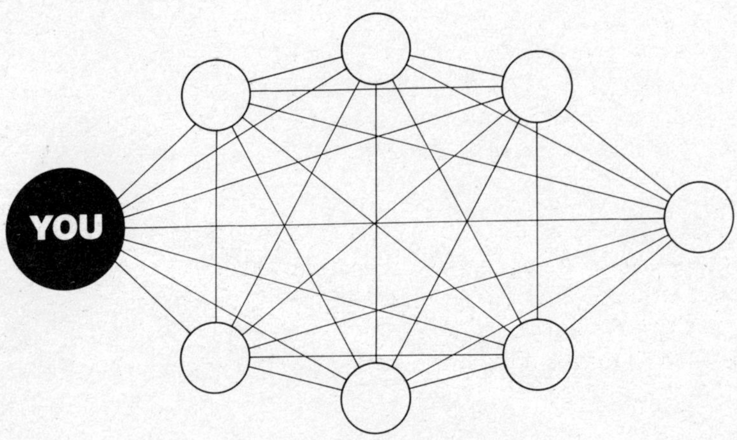

Figure 4.2
"Big fish, small pond" personal networks.

Either there are many cross-connections between the people whom you have links with (after the style of Figure 4.2), or there are none or only a few such cross-connections (like Figure 4.3). These alternative network patterns have very different meanings and implicit opportunities for what you may aspire to and how likely you are to get there.

If your personal network looks like the one shown in Figure 4.2, you have many cross-links or cross-connections. If

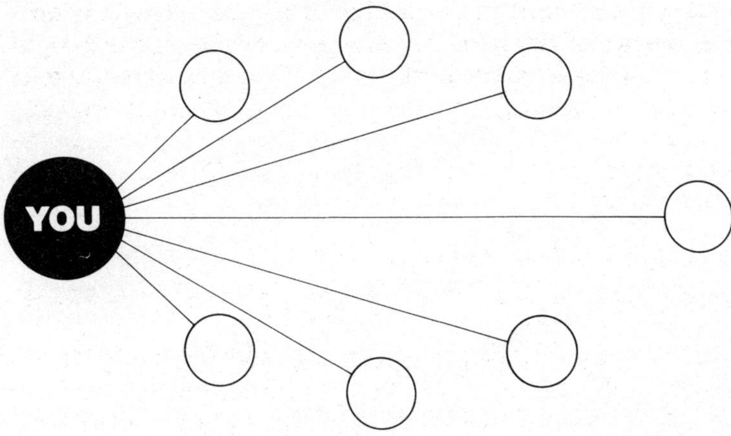

Figure 4.3
"Crossroads" or "distributed" personal networks.

you have 14* or more of the 21 possible cross-links, the chances are that you are fairly much a big fish in a small pond: the people whom you have links with are also in touch with each other. From your point of view, your contacts tend to be overlapped. They are much interconnected and form a supportive "clump" of relationships – that is, a close-knit personal network.

On the other hand, if you have drawn only a few or no cross-links on the diagram in Figure 4.1, it indicates that you have a more diverse or distributed type of linkage (like that shown in Figure 4.3). You do not have a close-knit personal network, at least not for this type of linkage. From your point of view, there is relatively little overlap in your personal network – your contacts are fairly much independent of each

---

* *Assuming a total of 'you' plus seven others, as shown in Figure 4.1. If you have varied this to be fewer or more than seven others, then assess whether you end up with two-thirds or more the total number of possible cross-links.*

other. You are linked across to others who, in turn, are probably connected in close-knit "clumps" of relationships to still others. That is, strategically you have access to various "ponds" or "clumps", and are in an advantageous position to plug into what's going on and to extend your effectiveness. To what extent you are advantageously placed in a "crossroads" position depends upon the next step.

If you have drawn only a very few or no cross-links in Figure 4.1 – that is, you have a crossroads pattern of direct links – then it becomes of particular interest to move a step still further out from where you are in the network. That is, to examine the personal networks of people you are in touch with, to see if their networks have close-knit or distributed patterns.

This extra step is important. The reason is that it allows you to see whether your personal network gives you the access you need to quite a number of small ponds that give breadth to the sorts of things you *can* know, and the range of contacts you *can* draw upon to achieve your objectives.

Turning to Figure 4.4, you should repeat the names or initials of the people from Figure 4.1 who are direct contacts of yours. Now take the first such person and write in the names of four or more people to whom that particular person is connected as far as you are aware (guess about who is linked to whom if necessary, and still use your same meaning of a relationship or link). Repeat this for all the other people with whom you are directly connected.

If many of the same names – say 18 or more of the 28 possible – keep recurring as contacts of the people who are directly connected to you, then from your point of view there is a good deal of overlap among your indirect contacts. They tend to be the same people; your contacts share many others with whom you do not have contact. This suggests that you are probably on the periphery of a larger close-knit clump or pond. You don't have direct links into it but you have good access through others, since you are connected by many

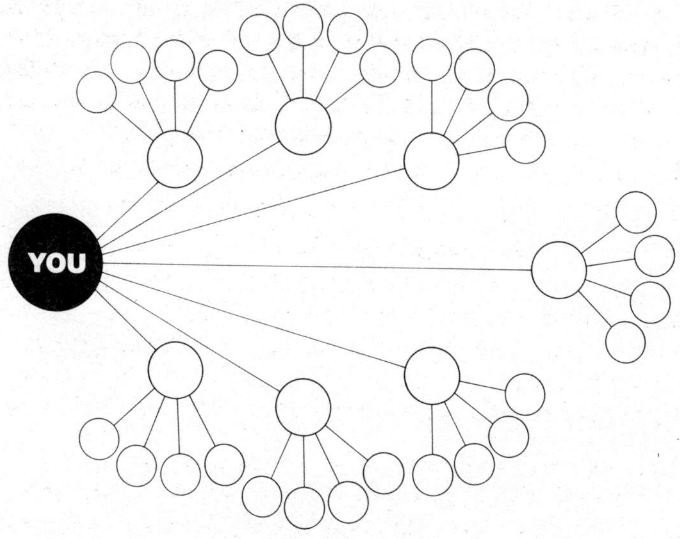

Figure 4.4
Indirect links – extending your personal networks.

(overlapped) indirect links. You are indirectly well connected into that pond, and if you know how to use those links effectively this could be an important resource for you.

If you have a distributed or crossroads pattern of links in Figure 4.1 (that is, after the style of Figure 4.3 such that your contacts are themselves *not* substantially cross-linked), then, if you are not on the periphery of a large pond, almost certainly you are strategically positioned in Figure 4.4 with linkage to numerous small ponds. In other words, if you don't have much overlap among your direct contacts – they are rather different sets of people – then it is unlikely that you will have much overlap among your indirect contacts.

The reason is simple. It is unlikely that your direct contacts will themselves have many people in common and yet themselves remain unconnected. For, as we shall discuss later, when two people share many third persons in common, the chances are high that the two people either are or will become directly linked themselves.

Table 4.1
How Does Your Network Look?

If your personal network (as in Fig. 4.1 is... • close-knit – then it looks like Fig. 4.2 or • distributed or crossroads – then it looks like Fig. 4.3 If your personal network is distributed or crossroads, then: either... • You are near the edge of a large pond and you are probably *in*directly well connected to it or • You are strategically positioned with linkage to numerous small ponds

A Consummate Networker

In 1970 Graeme, a clever accountant with an entrepreneurial flair, ran his own accounting practice and held part-time positions in two medium size businesses in which he held shares. In 1972 potentially serious charges were brought against him in the Supreme Court. The charges held the risk of affecting the future of his professional career and of damaging his financial future as well. The charges were malicious and partly politically motivated, since Graeme at the time was moving towards a political career in the Liberal Party, and some opponents within the party activated the dormant charges in order to knock him out of the race. Although there was no substance at all to the charges, the significance of Graeme's network in maintaining his morale during the trial and in giving evidence on his behalf contributed to his recovery and his future success.

Graeme's network of character witnesses extended across the spectrum of the major political parties, the professions, business and community service, and included a man who is now a bishop, another who became an Australian ambassador, and another who is now a Cabinet minister of the opposite political persuasion to Graeme's then alignment.

Graeme is a consummate networker and although these untimely events went against him initially, effectively ending any prospects of a political career in the short term; in the long term they worked in his favour. After he had been emphatically cleared, the government of the day later offered him a significant public service posting. Graeme believes the government's sense of fairness and the need to make up for a gross injustice partly motivated the offer, which he accepted. He is now a senior partner in a large international consulting firm, has many board appointments, has worked well with ministers from both major parties, and has been recognised in the Order of Australia. In spite of a number of personal adversities along the way, at 52 he is an outstanding success.

Graeme attributes his extensive network to his career mobility, which has over a lifetime included a number of different honorary appointments and employment postings from private business, government and academia. As well his willingness to take risks, his capacity to step out into the unknown and accept new challenges at various periods of his life, and to help others when requested have all continuously widened his field of contacts.

However, these contacts are not just ships passing in the night. There is both a natural outgoing art and a science to Graeme's use of his network. He is both a giver and a taker; many people owe him favours. He works instinctively and continuously on the basis of a helping reciprocity. He now knows from experience that what you give today tends to come back to you tomorrow or the day after or the day after that, and that it doesn't matter if there is never a direct reciprocation. Paradoxically and by way of illustration, the barrister on whose report the original court charges were made is now one of his clients, and the foreman of the jury later became his minister!

So far, two main points should have arisen in your network stocktaking and should also be obvious from Graeme's experience: you may have many or few links, and these links may be close-knit or distributed.

Many versus few links

You may have discovered how poorly or well connected you are in certain networks, in the sense of having few or many links. Somebody who is well connected in that they have many links has a far better chance of being in touch, having opportunities arise, knowing what is going on, or being able to manipulate the situation to their advantage – or, as in Graeme's case, saving your own bacon where necessary.

However, *the pattern of links is often more important* than the number of links, as was true in Graeme's situation.

Close-knit or distributed patterns of links

If the people you are in touch with (your direct contacts) are also largely in touch with each other, you are, in effect, a *big fish in a small pond*. Your personal network is close-knit in pattern and so is the pond ecology. You feel good. You probably feel part of a team and well supported, because of the overlapping linkage in your personal network. That is, many of the people you have contact with are also in touch with each other – there is a substantial degree of *shared* linkage.

On the other hand, if the people you are in touch with (that is your direct contacts) are mostly *not* in touch with each other, then you have a distributed linkage pattern – the chances are that you are strategically well placed with linkage to various small ponds.

The extent to which you are strategically well placed depends mostly upon how much cross-linkage there is among your indirect contacts, as indicated in Figure 4.4. If there is much indirect overlapping – that is your contacts share many other people in common but are not themselves linked directly between each other – you are probably located close to the boundary of a quite large grouping. Phis can occur, for example, after havinc moved to a new locality or a new job. However, if your direct contacts share many other people in common it is highly unlikely that they will remain unconnected directly themselves. Instead, it is almost certain that if you have a distributed pattern of linkage you are at the crossroads, and therefore strategically well positioned between various small groupings or ponds of people who interact largely with each other.

You have, in other words, access to a variety of ideas and alternative ways of viewing the world in various small ponds. You are not locked into one particular pond and perspective on what is important. This more distributed pattern of linkage, which is non-overlapping between your contacts, should be used to advantage to help achieve your objectives, and must be used to advantage if you are to be truly successful.

Checklist

Chapter 4

- Are you a big fish in a small pond? Taking stock of who you are connected to, and who they are connected to, is extremely important.
- Are the people with whom you are connected also mainly connected to each other? If so you are in a close-knit situation.
- If so, you also probably feel comfortable, but you might be locked out of other ideas and opportunities.
- The less interconnected, more diverse or distributed your patterns of relationships, the more you are likely to be strategically well placed for success.
- Small ponds are seductive because they are comfortable but there is a price to pay.

Chapter 5
Ah-ha, it is a Small World
Developing Relationships

The most powerful way to use your networks is to build on the common experiences that strengthen the bonds between you and others. It is so easy not to network in a deliberate fashion but to let relationships and contacts just evolve.

The ah-ha principle operates on sharing – the sharing of almost anything in common. Most often the things in common that will form the basis for a strengthening of bonds between people will be other people known in common and shared beliefs and values.

Shared People

Mary and Diana are introduced to each other at a cocktail party. The predictable scene will include some recounting of backgrounds and experiences, and as soon as one person in common is mentioned, the likely response will be "Ah-ha, so you know her too! When did you first meet her? What a small world it is!" And so on. Just as predictably, some recounting will follow of how each came to know this person jointly known, and this will lead to a second person in common, and then a third and perhaps a fourth. Several cocktails later they have discovered a significant number of people in common. And the more people in common that they have identified, that is, the more shared people between them, the higher the probability that they will find still other people whom they both know or know of. Most importantly, the more mutual links there are, the greater the chances of knowing each other in the first place; but, in any event, the potential tie between them is stronger.

Diagrammatically this can be shown as follows:

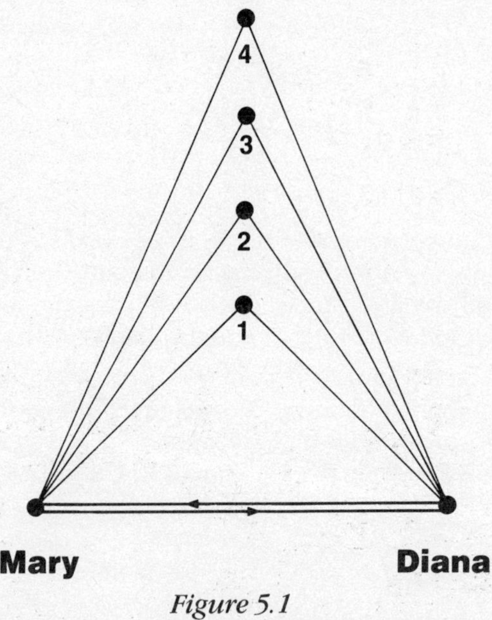

Figure 5.1
Shared People

If there is no direct relationship between Mary and Diana initially, then the more people they discover they share in common, the stronger the potential tie is between them.

Shared Experiences

In describing how she first met so and so, Mary might well recount travel or other experiences. The predictable reply is along the lines of: "Oh you visited Anchorage too! I thought it was marvellous, what did you think of it? Did you go to Vancouver?" Again, the more shared experiences or activities

AH... YOU MUST KNOW...
AH-HA, SO YOU KNOW...
AH-HA, YES... THEN YOU MUST KNOW...
AH-HA, THEN SURELY YOU KNOW...
YES...
OH GAWD... ...SHE'S MARRIED TO MY EX HUSBAND.....
KNIGHT

("Let me tell you about *my* operation"; "You are a keen trout fisherman too?"), or the more shared beliefs and values ("Tom is a fool, but his brother is great!"), the more the chances of those people meeting in the first place – they tend to move in the same circles. It *is* a small world, and the realisation of the points of commonality make it seem more so. They also, of course, make for more closely knit personal networks. To return to our theme, small close-knit ponds tend to be supportive because, by definition, the people are shared by virtue of their linkage and thus many other facets of life are also shared.

There are many pegs to hang our aspects of commonality on. It is this commonality that provides support for the self and perspectives of who I am and who I want to be, and also prevents confrontation with new ideas, different viewpoints, irrelevant experiences and so forth. We are all human and we all need feelings of closeness and belonging – we do not wish to denigrate the importance of such feelings in any way. But in the close-knit small pond, I am no longer me, no longer just the individual who makes up the "inner" self. I have subjugated my individuality to the shared extensions of self that make up the small pond. Not being exposed to all of the alternative viewpoints and cultural images of other ponds can be highly attractive and certainly very, very comfortable to fit in with. But it can be seductive as well as stifling and we each need to be aware of the situation.

Retreat

Our point here is that small ponds are terribly important as places for retreat, but not to live in or become trapped in forever and a day. It seems incredibly sad to think that many people will pass through their entire lives trapped in small, close-knit networks where nearly all the people they know also know each other. It is so nice and cosy that they will never know anything different, and the potential within them that could have been developed through a wider range of opportunities might lapse for want of a larger perspective on life and what it has to offer.

Recognising that you might be trapped in a small pond, that big fish status if the pond is small may be deleterious to your success, is the first step to doing something about it. The need to take stock of your networks is a crucial one if you are really going to succeed. Once your awareness has been raised to the necessity to become strategically placed at the crossroads in order to jump up to other ponds, the temptation to be lulled into a passive acceptance of big fish status will almost certainly disappear in favour of the delights and excitement of these other worlds.

Yet this does not mean abandoning the small pond. It is warm and comfortable, and nearly all of us need to be able to retreat to such a haven from time to time. It is not a matter of ditching previous small ponds; quite the contrary – they are crucial for identity and support reasons (Who am I? How am I doing?) and for a recharging of the batterics (Haven't you done well?). But one must go beyond them; get them in perspective and not be stifled by them. It must be a conscious, planned, deliberate move otherwise it is all too easy to stay put.

Big Fish in a Small Pond

The choosing of network contacts purposefully, and carefully fostering them in an achievement-oriented way, is a very different matter from letting things happen in a more or less laissez-faire fashion. All of us have personal networks, but not all of us realise that "network" is also a verb, so we can actually use our contacts. Most often our networks just evolve unconsciously, unpurposefully. Links are established that most often have the effect of serving to support our existing views, or at least not challenge too much what we already know and believe, or would like to.

Who am I? Since personal networks are extensions of the self, small ponds in effect become a mirror. A nice, safe, comfortable mirror. It feels great. It gives you and other big fish not only feelings of support and comfort but also a point of anchorage as to who you are and what you think – at least in the particular realm of this linkage activity. Who am I? I am the esteemed friend of all these people who often meet here on Friday nights or Sunday mornings. Who am I? I am someone who can swim in this small pond with unquestioned acceptance and even impudence. I can make a big splash and I can get away with it!

But you can also be incredibly vulnerable if those are the only contacts you have.

Networking to Get off the Reject Pile

One common problem many people face today in whatever sphere of activity they find themselves is unemployment. A few years ago we would not have dreamed that unemployment would hit the highly paid executive made redundant by restructures, mergers or other organisational adjustments. This is a relatively new phenomenon.

Most of these developments affect executives at upper and middle management in their forties and fifties and at this stage of life it is not easy to find employment. But senior executives have two things going for them – experience and contacts. Even so it takes real skill to use those contacts properly when looking for a new job in middle age and there are certain dos and don'ts associated with using close and interconnected networks that can mean the difference between success and failure.

The first advice Tim Heald in *Networks* gives to the redundant senior executive is "Don't talk to the neighbours, don't approach friends, don't panic, don't apply for jobs". The next advice is find a way to keep morale high. One way of doing this is to write down a list of achievements, put a résumé together and obtain appropriate references.

After that comes the important task of making a list of contacts that includes all your friends and acquaintances who might be able to recommend you for a job – then to pare that down in terms of priorities so that it becomes a smaller list of maybe 15.

Often the last employer will provide an outplacement agency to assist you with the above tasks, but if they don't the advice is to put the network, you have built up so carefully over the years, to work for you. In many ways you are now more vulnerable than you were when you were looking for your first job and for that reason you must use your personal networks very carefully.

Diverse Contacts

When the company for whom he worked was taken over by a large conglomerate, Gerry decided to quit the scene. At first Gerry felt depressed and didn't want his family to know he had left, but he finally took them into his confidence and they rallied supportively. His daughter, wife and son offered to make economies to their spending. His wife had, in fact, recently resumed her career and was earning a good wage, and took a promotion when it was offered her, something she may not have done if Gerry had been in a job. His son and daughter both took vacation jobs to augment the family income. This meant they took more responsibility, and it also meant that Gerry changed roles with his wife. He did the shopping and got the dinner – a role that might have been resisted had he still had a job. As it was, he welcomed the extra money his wife brought in and the extra time it bought him to look for the right job.

This financial breathing space and, more importantly, a feeling of emotional support was an enormous help, but Gerry knew he could not afford either psychologically or financially to stay out of the workforce for too long and he had to keep his contacts well oiled.

To avoid the impression that he was actively looking for a job, Gerry took a serviced office in an upmarket building, put up a consultant's shingle and had notepaper printed together with a small brochure featuring information about his background. Gerry obtained two small consultancy jobs and used those to maintain contacts and a presence around town. He was glad to have resisted the temptation to become semi-locked into the small pond in search of support, to pour out his troubles over endless glasses of beer with old friends. He was also glad he never once asked any of them directly for a job. He was surprised to find that a few of his closest friends were ultimately not his best contacts. They looked nervously in the other direction whenever the subject of employment was broached.

The most help came from more remote contacts who knew Gerry and his previous work. Although he was listed with several recruitment agencies, it was ultimately only after he had turned down several unsatisfactory job offers that the right opportunity arrived on his doorstep.This came through one of these third-hand contacts and, interestingly enough, actually through his old company.

Gerry is now chief executive in charge of a medium-sized company – his management skills are put to good use again and the value of his wider, more "distributed" personal networks is firmly etched in his mind. The experience of being on the outer has also given him a deeper understanding and sense of what is really valuable in life. This includes a new perspective on friendships, family, women's roles, colleagues and, indeed, the world. He is grateful for that experience and constantly puts it to new and creative use.

Locked In

By contrast, Diana relied solely upon her close-knit little pond rather than a wider set of contacts. Diana was a personnel officer with a large company. Her major support in recent years had come from associations in the feminist movement. Because she was young and inexperienced, she still had a lot to learn about the complexity of relationships in a large, male-dominated company. Many reforms needed to be made and she confronted management about her disquiet. Needless to say, they didn't listen and, in fact, they shot the messenger.

Diana chose to leave because they froze her out of any further discussion on any subject. She went straight to her small group of women contacts, most of whom were in the same kind of profession. She got lots of sympathy and emotional support but not much practical help.

The network started to feel threatened and vulnerable. Indeed they were. It took Diana a long time to make it back to a status similar to the position she had left behind. Not because she had a bad reputation but because she had not had the foresight to seek help in wider spheres or even to cultivate her contacts well beyond her supportive little group. Strategically she made the mistake of retreating back to the comfortable close-knit little pond where she again became virtually locked into the women's network and, indeed, a very small subset of that network. That made her feel good at the time but it did not really confront the inadequate networking problems she faced.

In the end she did an MBA and a wiser and better-educated Diana was recruited through one of her lecturers into another position with much better long-term prospects.

So if your job gets deleted and all your contacts are facing the same dilemma in their organisation – all have children the same age, mortgages to pay off or are studying in nightschool – you could be in trouble. We are all equally vulnerable if we have few contacts outside our own circle and the older we grow together the more vulnerable we become.

Building Contacts

Bill began to realise the dangers inherent in this situation nearly 20 years ago. At the age of 41 he became aware of the longer-term situation. He saw old people living in lonely retirement, many of their friends gone and no further challenges left in their lives. In a culture of the young, attitudes to old people are fraught with stereotypical beliefs that lock old people out of opportunities in much the same way as women are locked out in male-dominated cultures.

Bill started to develop and build new networks. Before that he was contentedly and comfortably locked into a network of associations and people more or less his own age. They attended college together, dispersed into the workforce at the same time and rose through their organisations, variously helping each other or not as the case might be. By the time Bill turned 45 some of his contemporaries had retired early and a few had even died.

Once he realised how locked in he had become, he deliberately set about building contacts among younger people who would still be around in positions of authority and power, long after his own age group had relinquished their hold on both. As the marketing director of a large company he had a busy job, but in his leisure time he built up knowledge and skill in another area, horticulture, something that had always interested him.

Information about Bill's interest in horticulture spread among his work colleagues. He regularly contributed articles on plants and gardens to the staff newsletter, and established links with people who had similar interests in companies with which he dealt on a day-to-day basis. In addition both Bill and his wife attended national horticultural conferences in their spare time and served on several subcommittees. They also made a study of who made decisions about landscape contracts in government departments and companies when new plants and offices were being planned.

So when Bill retired from his company two years ago, aged 60, he did so with the contract for landscaping his former employer's new office complex in one hand and a retirement benefit package in the other. Now 62, he is the managing director of his own company – a thriving successful business.

Bill used his knowledge of the entrenched cultural attitudes to the aged in a positive and directed way. He built up links across age groups. He understood that power for some diminishes with age (unless you are Ronald Reagan, of course), and good contacts and relationships with young people on the way up would ensure a continuity of that access. Those people were also grateful to have access to Bill's knowledge and expertise about marketing as well as horticulture – knowledge that he shared quite liberally.

He also figured out how decisions are made in his newfound area of interest while he was still within the company structure, and he learned about how contracts are awarded and by whom. He built an image or reputation in the field so people believed in his competence and he wasn't afraid to take a risk, moving into something new when others his age were winding down their own operations.

Supportive feelings derived from membership of a close-knit social network are bought at a price. For living in a small pond is very limited. One is constrained to seeing things in certain ways, and exposed to new ideas and new opportunities in a highly selective fashion. It can even be difficult to bump into alternative viewpoints casually; they are just not around. And attempts to peep outside the pond or break out of the mould (this is not a mixed metaphor; surely you have seen a fish mould) are likely to be met with "iron curtain" sanctions – the iron curtain can be rung down most severely. You know your place.

As we all attempt to achieve our goals, one of the most difficult things to do is to try to move ahead of where our friends are. Or, more generally, to move ahead of where our closely knit network colleagues are (who are often not necessarily friends). Hence, one's friends and contemporaries in any close-knit networks can act as a brake on forward-looking and achievement-oriented movement.

The solution? You *have* to jump up to another pond. But read on before you do so.

Making the Jump

Essentially you have a three-way choice. *Firstly*, you may remain locked in, blinkered and constrained by a small pond. You may be very much aware of this, yet deliberately choose this course of action because the warmth and supportiveness of the close-knitted network appeals to your needs to belong, feel wanted and comfortable in relations with others. In making this choice you are aware that you may be limiting your opportunities for wider sources of knowledge and, in effect, be abdicating your freedom to really decide what is going on. You give the decision processes over to the group to an extent, but that is the cost and you recognise it (see Chapter 9, "Network Liberation in the Information Society"). You are also aware that you are vulnerable in hitching your wagon to this close-knit little star in that you have not got the wider linkages you may need if changes in fortune occur either for yourself or for the group as a whole.

Secondly, you may decide to jump up to another pond. Perhaps to jump up to several other ponds more or less at the same time, or else to one particular pond and then another, and then another and so on along some assumed stream that is like a critical path among various activities leading toward goal attainment. The sequential pattern of pond jumping or the jumping to one particular pond depends upon the larger strategy that you have in mind, the objectives that you have set yourself. Then your pond-jumping decisions are really responses to those strategic objectives, as part of fitting in, tailoring and otherwise realigning your network structures to fit your strategies. You can have a great strategy with all sorts of well-thought-out objectives, but will your network structures, your actual patterns of contact, allow you to achieve them? If not, you will need to build your links and plan your pond jumping accordingly.

Thirdly, you may decide to jump up not to any particular pond or ponds but to what we term an "information brokerage" role because it connects you into numerous small ponds. This is potentially the most rewarding because you are then strategically positioned at the cross roads between various small ponds, but not locked into any one particular pond and the provinciality of views that may prevail there. But it is also potentially a tenuous and difficult choice for some people. This is because of the inherent lack of support/comfort afforded that comes with dwelling in just one small pond and because of the balancing routines that you necessarily have to perform from time to time with people from different ponds pushing and pulling in different directions. However, the brokerage role puts you in an advantageous position. You are virtually at the crossroads and have access to a diversity of knowledge and opportunities. It may be that you choose this strategic position between ponds for certain purposes, not forever and a day but merely as a prelude to jumping up into the "right" pond. On the other hand, if you choose to stay at the crossroads and work that brokerage situation correctly you are almost assured of success.

Information Brokerage Where It Suits

People who take a role outside their own professional life are acting to some degree as information brokers. For example, Sol Encel, professor of sociology at the University of New South Wales, has developed a network of contacts outside academia that gives him access to many different ponds and that positions him to play the brokerage role where it suits. He has been involved in educational planning for schools (the Education Commission); in telecommunications committees (Telecom Towards 2000); in futures conferences and in science and technology committees. His advice to people in similar circumstance is to take the opportunity when it's offered – to remember why you personally want to be involved, to maintain your own identity and to remember the reasons why others have asked you to be involved. Your expertise will be an asset if you do not try to change your identity and become something you are not.

Be finely grounded in who you are, then your objectivity will be trusted. Brokers must be trusted, otherwise their brokerage role effectiveness will eventually decline.

In the building of links, Sol and the others know that the ah-ha experience is extremely important. The ah-ha experience comes with the joy of mutual recognition and commonality ("You know Fred too!" or "Yes, Hamilton Island is marvellous!"). It is so rewarding to have the affirmation of others that it seems the things you are doing with your life must be O.K. and the things the other person is doing with their life must be O.K., because you know the same sorts of people, you have been to the same sorts of places and are into the same sorts of experiences.

Using the principle of ah-ha experiences, you can build links into new small ponds by working away at shared perspectives and later reinforcing them over a period. In effect, what you are doing is making it *seem* to be a small world. You are simulating the culture of the small pond that you desire to be tapped into. This is done by referring to the points of commonality that represent the shared understandings within that small world. By the use of ah-ha experiences, you can then bring the small world in closer to you and your new contacts. The net result of this sharing of understandings, based upon commonalities, is that each of us becomes embedded in networks of linkages evolved over time upon sharing with others in a comfortable fashion all sorts of ah-ha experiences. The sharing feels good. Life is comfortable. Indeed, it is a small world.

Checklist

Chapter 5

- Are you subjugating your individuality to the small pond, thus denying yourself new opportunities and ways of thinking about the world?
- Extending your networks away from the small pond does not mean abandoning those contacts. They are essential for support and identity.
- But larger and more diverse ponds can also get you out of trouble, like unemployment in middle age.
- The older you grow together with your tight-knit group, the more vulnerable you become.
- But you can build links across into other small ponds by the use of ah-ha experiences that make things seem to be part of a small world.

Chapter 6

The Psychology of the Small Pond

Reinforcement of Your Ideas – It Feels Good

We are not victims of the world we see, we are victims of the way we see the world. If that world feels comfortable, then take another look.

There are no six easy steps to guarantee success, let alone one easy step as implied by many "success" books. By the time you check yourself to be sure you are thinking positively or open the kit bag to get out the right "formula", the opportunity has passed. Access is needed to a variety of opportunities; you need relationships, links "on tap", to get to the right places at the right time. Furthermore, you need a variety of informational inputs beyond the scope of a comfortable close-knit circle of contacts made up of people who share similar values and who have the same or similar sorts of ideas.

"Like" Talks to "Like"

People don't organise themselves in a random way. It occurs selectively and largely according to least effort on a similarity basis; "like" talks to "like". It's easier that way. And it's psychologically more rewarding to plug into conversations where we hear much of our own views reflected in what is said. It is the shared, common elements of interest that gratify and that underlie our choice in communication partners. Not usually, of course, in any overt, deliberate choice-making sense; instead, for most of us it just happens.

The net result of this "non-choice" but quite patterned set of contacts and, therefore, channels of information, is reinforcement of our own ideas. The information environment of each of us as individuals at the centre of it becomes limited in terms of what *has* been gleaned – the attitudes formed ("This is the way to do things around here!") – and is limiting in terms of what can be done, what opportunities and ideas can be learned.

Berger's and Luckman's book on *The Social Construction of Reality* examines the relationships between human thought and the social context in which it arises. This concept provides a number of explanations about how and why people's thinking is limited when their social interactions are restricted. Social interaction determines the access we have to knowledge and how we screen that knowledge. Our understanding of a certain situation can be limited by our preconceptions and by the values we hold. Bev's (Chapter 1) view of the world was expanded by the group she worked for. This meant she screened information differently and her perceptions were changed as a result. It also changed her attitudes and later it changed her behaviour.

Richard Bergland in his book *The Fabric of Mind*, traces the history of some scientific and medical ideas from Aristotle to the present day. The fascinating thing about Bergland's book is his description of the way in which certain vital knowledge was locked up for centuries because it didn't fit the preconceptions of the time. One of Bergland's chapters is titled "The First Old Boy's Network" – the network perpetrated what now appears to us to be ridiculous notions of how the body works and it held the practice of medicine back for nearly 2000 years. Aristotle's notion was that an ether-like substance descended from heaven into the arteries of man (quintessence) and this was the life-giving force. To suggest that blood circulated around the body was heresy. To illustrate how entrenched this idea became in every day language, women's fainting fits in Victorian times were called a "fit of the vapours".

This "universal truth" of quintessence was perpetrated as doctrine by Alexander the Great, a devoted disciple of Aristotle who locked up this intellectual property in the libraries of Egypt and who brooked no discussion as to its veracity. An unquestioning acceptance ensured linking quintessence with religious teaching about God and the nature of the universe, and thus through the centuries this notion became carved in stone.

The intellectual chicanery of a man named Galen who had more accurate evidence contradicting this view 550 years after Alexander the Great also ensured the longevity of this mistaken idea. It was not until William Harvey's publication on the circulation of blood in 1628, that the belief in Aristotle's quintessence notion was seriously questioned. But by then the times were right for that questioning to accelerate, since the 17th century was a rich period for scientific and philosophical thought. The absolute hold of old religious dogma had also been shaken by that time.

As this case illustrates, "like" talking to "like" tends towards consensus. Think of the various groups that you belong to. Professional groups get together to bathe in the same pond; supervisors do, top managers do, housewives do and farmers do; and the same age groups, churches, clubs and car pools all are reasons for association, for commonality. Sharing of some sort, including a commonality of acquaintances ("You know Joe too!"), makes for meaningful discussion, for bells that really "ring", for a good feeling. And known pathways are a lot easier than battling to find new common ground.

Of course, there has to be some variety of content to keep you involved. But essentially many statements are overlapping, modified and adapted restatements of the basic viewpoints held in common, such that the process of "like" talks to "like" becomes similar to looking into an infinite series of less-than-perfect mirrors. Particular views of reality circulate and, not unlike Aristotle's views, can become virtually universal truths. The pathways, many and varied in theory, become, unwittingly and selectively, well trodden in practice and no-one dares question the accepted wisdom. Seventes was burnt at the stake in 1553 for suggesting blood circulated around the body. Galileo's experiments on gravity and his belief in heliocentricity kept him out of favour with the Catholic Church until very recent times.

In more contemporary terms a number of studies have tracked the way the leaders of our large organisations spend their time, and how they get their information. Most of them talk only to top management and to each other. Most don't have time to read much. Most reinforce each other's vision of the world – they drink at the same clubs, they live in similar suburbs, their children go to similar schools. An article in the *Australian* on 21 May 1984 entitled "Who's Playing the Board Game", revealed that of some 950 public companies, two people hold 13 directorships, one person holds 11 and three people hold nine. The article also revealed that, according to one confidential survey, more than 40 per cent of the total sample of directors hold interlocking directorships – too much cross pollination. As one critic, Geraldine Paton, put it, "Too many boards are made up of the same people of the same age and of similar backgrounds."

No doubt directors and managers feel comfortable talking to each other; but is it good for them or for the world for that to continue, and can we trust them when they ask us to follow them over the top when we know that their knowledge really comes from such a small and often stagnant pool? Perhaps this is an understandable process. But in the extreme it feeds upon itself. The way we perceive things selectively according to our predispositions and, in parallel, choose our communication contacts selectively, means that limits can become set for us as to who we are, what we can think and what we can do. And it is oh so comfortable to go down this track – or to stay there.

In Chapter 9 on network liberation we explore why at the present time in the information society this is such a dangerous situation. We are at a crossroads. We cannot go back.

Historical perspectives like those offered by Bergland provide new, important ones – new understandings, new ideas. This provides the framework for a paradigm shift that will allow us to expand to the challenges and values of the future.

In summary, it is the hammer of convenient and conventional social contacts that nails us to a position, to particular ways of viewing the world and what it offers. As we said at the beginning, we are not victims of the world we see, we are victims of the way we see the world. And the way we see the world depends in large measure upon whether we live in a small pond of comfortable contacts or a larger world of wider and often not-so-comfortable contacts.

Are You Comfortable?

The well-trodden pathways of contacts assume an especially comfortable feeling when the people you know also mostly know each other. You share friends, business contacts or whatever. This sociability ethic, has to a fair extent, become a moral imperative that is to be found in every suburb, every city, every day. Listen to the talk. Same people, same topics, same circulation of viewpoints. Occasional ventures to other larger or different ponds, followed by hasty retreats to the comfort of small ponds. The status quo is preserved.

Attempts to deviate, to break the unwritten "rules" of what to say in the small pond invite the iron curtain treatment. This curtain is rung down perhaps even more often when accidental gaffes are committed rather than planned deviance, either following a period of absence or on first arrival when personal links are not established and other links are not known. A new job or a new suburb are classic situations for accidental gaffes to be made and for the iron curtain treatment to be given. In either situation, one of the first things to be done is to discover the lay of the land as to who associates with whom and, most importantly, who doesn't!

This exercise in deducing the network configurations also entails finding out what the prevailing attitudes and values are in different parts of the overall network, quite apart from the question of judiciously establishing one's own personal links. In a new community or one that has changed, ignorance of the current state of the network can generate results like walking over a minefield without a mine detector. If you are not careful... Boommm!

"Like" Seeks Out "Like"

Both authors of this book spent time living in the country and both of our experiences there have influenced this book. Anne went to live in the country as a young wife. She was full of enthusiasm and keen to participate in the life of the community. But she found herself confronted by a very conservative culture. There were not many allies for this uppity young woman from the city who gratuitously started throwing her weight around, but eventually she found the allies.

One such was a man called Allen. One of four sons who all lived on properties close to one another and who had made it through sheer hard work, determination, grit and extreme frugality. Although they were smart they were very closed in, poorly educated and extremely conservative. All except Allen, who came to be Anne's ally in the parents' and citizens' movement. They went off to many meetings together since they were both on the district council and once a month had to travel 70 or 80 kilometres to meetings together.

Why was Allen's perspective so different from his brothers and from many of the other members of the community? Allen was an ex-serviceman and during the war, while his brothers were shearing the district's sheep, Allen was travelling the world, meeting people, discussing other things far removed from farming, and facing death in the jungles of New Guinea.

Allen wasn't the only one, of course. There was a distinct difference between those who had gone away and those who hadn't. There was even a difference in the new generation who were attending high schools sixty kilometres from their homes and mixing with young people from the bigger towns

– those who were sent to boarding school were even more sophisticated and independent. They came from wealthier families so of course their choices were very much greater.

It is not easy, however, to make the transition from one pond to another. Every group has its own culture – a subject we explore in greater detail in Part II. Groups, nations, organisations and people living in particular geographic territories structure themselves, their beliefs, systems and values towards maintaining stability, cohesion and power. It is important to understand this before you rush in, as Anne did as a young bride, to take them by storm.

Ceilings on Achievement

These small ponds are comfortable because of similarities of viewpoint and because full membership is not freely granted but is hard won over a period of time. Once in, support and the enhancement of one's identity "naturally" follow because of the ease of interaction and the reinforcing nature of it. Life has fewer uncertainties; it becomes more patterned, more predictable. Such characteristics are typical of rural and remote-area settlements the world over, but are by no means confined to such communities. For the research chemist in New York, the housewife in Los Angeles, the company executive in Sydney, or the stockbroker in London, life has pattern and predictability in terms of the regular and frequent contacts each has with others who serve as major sources of reinforcement and mutual support.

Perhaps most of us are in a small pond and have a need to be. To succeed, however, it is necessary to recognise what constitutes a small pond and what doesn't and whether or not the small ponds set ceilings on what can be achieved.

If you feel particularly comfortable and complacent, the chances are that you are a relatively big fish in a small pond. Do you need to jump up to a larger pool to realise your objectives? If not, why not? Is there perhaps an element of fear of leaving the known, the predictable, the well trodden, to embrace the unknown? This is understandable, but the stark reality is that many success stories can be attributed to examining, ajd then more effectively managing, personal networks to provide access to new contacts that can help achieve personal goals.

And if you do decide to jump up to other ponds, we suggest you learn to read the cultural ways of the group you wish to access. Developing an understanding of the dynamics of each of those settings will be crucial to your understanding of how these linkages operate, what new perceptions and ideas they have to offer you, or how the people there restrict their own reality. The cross cultural aspects of the pond-jumping are discussed further in Part II and are linked to the way in which we perceive the world and the behaviour that flows from those perceptions.

Checklist

Chapter 6

- There are no easy formulas to guarantee success.
- The name of the game is to build up relationships so you have links on line when you need them.
- Reinforcement of our ideas may feel good, but if that is all we have we never expand our knowledge.
- "Like" talking to "like" tends towards consensus.
- Our social interactions influence our perceptions of reality.
- There are important historical lessons to be learned from the past about the dangers of being locked in.
- We are on the brink of a paradigm shift and the beginning of new ways of thinking about the world.
- Close-knit communities don't necessarily warmly welcome people who are different.

Chapter 7

Locked into Z-Ville, Locked out at Y-Ville

Closely-Knit Personal Networks can Make or Break Your Chances of Success

Personal Encounters in Z-Ville

As an author of this book, I (John) would like to share with you some personal experiences of networking. These experiences changed my life and affected the way I viewed the world.

I had always had an interest in rural life although I originally came from the city. As a child I had spent vacations on people's properties. What had really impressed me was the friendliness and support that country people offered. Being in a rural area to me was like living in a "real" community of very much shared interests. A key observation about this supportive environment was that the same things that I was interested in also seemed to interest most others.

The idea of living in a "community of interests" was so attractive that on leaving school I decided to become a "jackaroo". Now in Australia a jackaroo ("jillaroo" is the female equivalent) is like an apprentice on a country property or outback sheep or cattle station. He aspires to become a manager. I was interested in sheep and cattle and also the farming side of things, keenly interested. But it really wasn't a matter of a deeply held concern for things rural. Rather, it was the case that I needed to take an interest in things rural if I was to be an accepted part of the close-knit community. And there was no half way membership – you were either in it or out of it!

Like-minded people talk mainly to one another. It is easier that way, it is friendlier. In a small country town most of the people you know also know one another. They therefore tend to share the same sorts of views; similar information is circulated around and around. That is not to say that they do not have differences of opinion. Differences do occur, but they tend to be variations of opinion on the same themes rather than distinctly different perspectives. It is easier to go along with whatever are the currently held views, not because of a rational decision to do so but because the information environment is such that one can hardly be exposed to any other views – not consistently or persistently at least. Life is simply easier. It is not necessarily a cop-out, it is just the way most of us let things happen. And it is friendlier that way, because your cherished views are nurtured and supported far more often than they are challenged.

Locked into Z-Ville

Having joined a "community of interests", all looked well for the present, if not the future (and why worry about the future?). The people in my district mostly knew me. They were almost extensions of me. We played tennis together, we went to parties together, we played football together, we went to the same bars together – and so on, frequently. The bonds of commonality were strengthened. We shared the same ideas. In fact, the term "we" meant that we shared the same people – the contacts of any one of us were also the contacts of each other. We were a very tightly knit and highly supportive little community.

With hindsight it is easy to see the dangers. The tightly knit community was so supportive that it was stifling in terms of development. It nearly suffocated me. I was like a horse wearing blinkers – I could look neither too far to the left nor to the right. I was hemmed in to particular ways of viewing the world, and understanding who I was and what life was supposed to be about. But the frightening thing is that it was so close-knit and therefore so supportive that it was blinding. I had to get out of that community but I couldn't recognise that I had to get out – because I was lulled into its ease, convenience and friendship, its close-knit character was uncomfortably comfortable!

My mother had frequently insisted that I enroll in a university course (by correspondence since I lived in the outback). "University", I said to her, "you're joking!" But to keep her quiet I took the minimum number of subjects. It was extremely difficult to find the time for study given my schedule of sport and revelry. She was persistent fortunately, and eventually shamed me into actually completing a few subjects.

Somewhere through my study of a variety of topics that lifted me out of my local community, the light dawned – I had been one of several big fish in a small pond, and I could never grow to become a really big fish until I jumped up into a bigger pond. I loved my small community. The relationships I made there were much valued and I still stay in touch with a few people. But it was so close-knit and too comfortable; it nearly suffocated me.

Innovation Barriers

The close-knitted network also prevented innovation and the opportunities to adopt new methods. On a stud sheep property, the stud master or the classer is the judge and arbiter as to what bloodlines will be developed and the particular features that will be emphasised across the years through selection of appropriate stock. Will straight backs, wide horns or "bright" wool be emphasised? But how were the selection criteria evolved? What "ponds" of knowledge did the stud masters dip into in order to decide the future of (at that time) Australia's number one export earning industry?

I recall most vividly the late Harry O'Brien, one of the nation's top classers, telling me to "Hit him with the raddle boy!", which meant that I had to mark a ram with a piece of coloured chalk to show the ram as accepted or rejected, or put into this grade or that grade. All too often, it seemed to me, a ram was accepted if it had such features like a "bright eye" or a "good upturn in the horn", which gradually dawned on me to be only tenuously connected to the business of growing wool. Surely the length, colour and quality of wool were at least as important as look in the eye or curl of the horn!

The top sheep from the various studs were regularly exhibited at sheep shows in the major cities. Stud masters congregated there and talked mainly with other stud masters. This, of course, had a reinforcing effect on what were "correct" and "acceptable" views and simultaneously served to prevent alternative views from gaining a foothold. From the vantage point of hindsight it is obvious that the net result was development of a close-knit self-congratulatory cocoon that was difficult to penetrate with logic.

The University of New South Wales had been trying to get wool measurement and testing services off the ground for years. However, in the bush – at the coalface, so to speak – you rarely heard of such ideas. And if any ideas had managed to get through on the bush telegraph they would have been attributed to a bunch of city wimps.

The strategy of improving wool by selecting for "curl in the horn" was supported by the close-knit network structures of stud masters talking mainly to other stud masters. These structures were so circumspect and reinforcing of existing views that other strategies could hardly get a look-in. In a sense, the structure dictated the strategy rather than the other way around.

The sequel to this story is that eventually wool testing did gain wider acceptance but it took over 20 years and a new generation of stud masters and classers.

The recognition of being nearly stuck in Z-Ville forever and a day, revelling in but nonetheless oppressed by tight-knit networks, was something that spurred me on to try to understand how it is that people evolve and fashion their networks, which then can tend either to constrain them or to give them the opportunities for liberation. These Z-Ville experiences directly influenced my desire to write this book. For the interesting thing is that network building for most of us occurs unconsciously and almost never in a systematic way. Taking stock of who we are connected with and whether we are so placed that we really can achieve our goals (will our structure let us implement our strategies?), does not usually occur consciously. Yet if you look about, you will find that the most successful people in life are highly skilled networkers – they do take stock of their network structures and see that they are appropriate and then network their way to success.

Personal Encounters in Y-Ville: The Iron Curtain Treatment

After Z-Ville, I guess I was wary about getting trapped in tightly knit little networks again, and because of that considered that the wide world of television and radio would be a contrast to Z-Ville and the outback.

It sure was different but I was wrong. There were *still* tightly knit little networks, plenty of small ponds each built around various small concerns and each with their own big fish. Z-Villes everywhere! I hadn't reckoned on city life being just as cliquey. And yet it is obvious when you think about it – tightly knit little networks exist in the most cosmopolitan of urban environments, and although lacking in visibility they can be every bit as stifling for personal development as living in a close-knit rural community.

The broadcasting company that employed me sent me to Canberra. It is a planned city dominated by government employees arranged into structures like layers of a large sponge cake. The formal structures create this situation but the informal structures maintain and embellish them. Different patterns of connections permeate every aspect of life in Canberra. Division 4 people talk mainly to division 4 people, division 5 people talk mainly to division 5 people, and so on. And, just as day follows night, the attitudes that are held and the social acceptance patterns follow the different patterns of connections that people weave across the formal structure.

At first it was hell. I didn't know anybody and it was virtually impossible to break in. There were plenty of parties and social activities but they did not include me. People at each bureaucratic layer of the sponge cake seemed to have parties for people on the same or similar layer. The trouble was it was extraordinarily difficult to get included in the first place. It was like an iron curtain that could come down with considerable force to clamp you out. The only way to get onto the other side was to be invited by somebody who was already part of that internal network and a good networker to boot.

Once in, you were there on probation. There was a welcoming with open arms, as long as one had contacts or other known third parties in common, or had experiences in common (for example, skiing) or places in common (You were in Saigon too!). In those cases it was possible to forge real links that would allow a fuller acceptance. Otherwise, at the end of the probationary period, that damned iron curtain would be rung down again, sometimes losing an arm or a leg in the process. I eventually made it. Four months after arriving in Canberra I was as bad as everybody else. I belonged in my own cliques, and I was damn well going to stay there and shut out any crazy individual who was impertinent enough to try to break into *my* circle of contacts.

Coping with Being Locked out

By contrast, let us move outside the sphere of Canberra and see how somebody else coped in a very different situation.

Frank, head of a government department in one of the States, enjoyed a high profile in his own right, but this was exaggerated because of his association with an innovative and high flying minister. When the government changed after many years it was time to lock people out. A departmental head who had too high a profile associated with the previous political regime was systematically targeted for removal. This was the ideal opportunity for little people to settle old scores of one kind or another. Whether the people were talented and loyal to the government or not they were ignominiously removed from their positions and forced to find other jobs within the government. Some left the service altogether seeking employment elsewhere – others stayed and stagnated with little to do with their time – "the living dead".

If this had happened in Canberra they would have had no option but to leave or at least bide their time in a back room until the government changed again. But in the larger pond Frank's energy and his capacity to use his old contacts well and to develop new ones meant that his considerable talents were able to be used effectively. During the hiatus period between being moved sideways and finding a new role, Frank gained some formal recognition in management training and undertook the administrative training of hundreds of senior- and middle-level officials within a new agency to which he had become attached for another consulting task. Trainees ranged from very senior to quite junior officials.

The result of this first 12 months' work brought him into contact with a sizeable cross section of people throughout the department, and several other agencies asked him to run similar courses for their senior executives. His network, which had previously been in the Education Department and related services, was thus quickly extended and from there across other departments. Entirely new spheres of influence were opened to him.

Ultimately he was offered a significant appointment as a troubleshooter or special reorganisational or review and reform assignments and a trailblazer in new areas of government activity, a kind of internal high-level government consultant who could think creatively and deal with problems creditably at all levels.

Through this system he has also identified a network of innovative thinkers within the public service and related fields since his own personal reputation and success also depends on their cooperation. When a new and developing task involves them, it is in his interests and in the interests of the network for them all to keep in touch with each other on a regular basis.

However, Frank's activities extend well beyond the public service. He has been involved over the years in sport and youth activities, in Rotary, local government and services for disabled people, on a voluntary basis. This involvement has brought him into close contact with many people in the business community and, since his current assignment includes strong and joint cooperation between business and government, these contacts have proved immensely valuable.

Frank was locked out; in no uncertain terms he received the iron curtain treatment. But in his indomitable way he coped with the problem. He attributes his success both to a capacity to stretch out and take risks and to his many contacts in ever-widening spheres. Even though circumstances forced this situation, Frank turned adversity to advantage.

So What?

It is clear as crystal – there are three basic situations. *Firstly*, many people are unconsciously trapped in tightly knit networks. They will pass through their entire lives feeling psychologically comfortable and well supported by acquaintances, colleagues and friends but never really succeeding. They can't. They are locked into particular avenues and limited opportunities as surely as if they were locked in jail. Sadly, very few people can recognise how their development is being stifled because they feel so comfortable. If you feel comfortable, beware! Tightly knit personal networks tend to be supportive of what you already believe and therefore comfortable and easy to live with but highly insidious. They often serve to mask even the beginnings of recognition of genuine alternatives and real opportunities.

Secondly, there are many people who are locked out, who are on the edge of tightly knit groups and various communities – yet who want with all their hearts to be embraced (and even suffocated) in a tightly knit personal network, to be one of the in crowd, one of the mob. How do you forge the links that extend you, through your personal networks, in the direction you want to go? Firstly, you have got to recognise what your current pattern of relationships looks like, that is, take stock (see Chapter 4, "Big Fish in Small Ponds"), and then network your way to achieve your objectives (see Chapter 8, "Achieving Your Personal Objectives").

Thirdly, many people struggle through much of their lives to build a "community of interests", to pull people together from disparate backgrounds to work together or to play together, to build a tightly knit organisation, association or community (these days it is probably called a network). How does one do this? Some of those people will be locked in and therefore constrained in their opportunities for contribution and development; and some will be locked out and therefore also constrained in their opportunities for contribution and development. Either way, the actual networks that people have evolved must be examined as a step prior to determining how things should be changed to improve the "community of interests".

Each of the above types of situation must be confronted if one is to succeed. Frank, for example, had the tools for survival at his disposal when things went wrong. He knew intuitively and his experience had shown already that success happens not independently of others but through and with others. "Network" can be a verb as well as a noun. To network your way to success means to manage your networks. But you first need to know what they are, to take stock, to take inventory. Who am I connected to? Where am I locked in? Where am I locked out? How can I extend myself through and with others? But all of this networking has to happen in relation to goals, objectives, a decision to develop more positive attitudes, improved self-images and so on. These are crucial and are, of course, the more conventional and individualistic components that go to make up that elusive thing called success. In the next chapter we show you how to marry these two components or dimensions of success: to set goals and objectives and network your way to the key people who can influence the achievement of your goals. The two dimensions are essential. Reliance upon individualistic concerns like the setting of objectives requires a network strategy to make the objective realisable – to allow you to jump up to the right ponds and to avoid being locked in or locked out of situations that prevent goal attainment.

Checklist

Chapter 7

- In Z-Ville, individuals reinforced each others' views – it was easier, friendlier and more comfortable that way.

- Close-knit patterns of supportive ties meant that it was very difficult for new ideas, new ways of doing things, to gain credence. The status quo was preserved. Life was comfortable and remained so.

- But people can be locked-in to tightly-knit little networks in metropolitan situations. Y-Ville was just like a small rural community. There were people both locked-in and locked-out.

- Take stock of your personal networks. They may not provide you with the opportunities you want nor the insurance you need against changes in fortune.

- There are three basic situations: (1) many people are comfortable yet unaware that they are trapped in tightly knit networks, (2) others feel locked out of them, and (3) still others want to devote their lives to building networks of common interest.

Chapter 8
Achieving your Personal Objectives
Where Do You Want to Go and How Are You Going to Get There?

"If you don't know where you are going," as Lawrence Peters once said "you are sure to end up somewhere else." In Chapter 2 we argued that success is a matter not only of "fixing your head up" – that is, developing the right psychological approach, setting objectives, developing a positive mental attitude and so forth – it is also a matter of taking stock of your personal networks and ensuring that you have the right connections that can allow you to achieve those objectives. It is like the old horse and cart problem. It is no good having the cart full of all sorts of bright ideas, objectives and positive mental attitudes if the network horse is not there to pull it, or wants to pull it in the wrong direction.

Stated differently, your strategies for life fulfilment will not and cannot work properly without the right network structures to allow you to get there. The strategies that you develop have to be accompanied by appropriate structures. Strategies and structures have to go hand in hand, to be dovetailed. This chapter shows you how to put these two things together. Essentially it boils down to: "Where do you want to go?" (strategic concerns, like the objectives you set for yourself) and "How are you going to get there?" (your personal network structures along with your other resources like money and so on). We cannot overemphasise that a close fit between these two elements of success is crucial.

Spheres of Activity

We all wear different "hats" at different times. You might be a manager, homemaker, owner, employee, professional, mother, father, golfer, tennis player, friend, lover and so on at different times and in different circumstances (hopefully!). Ken, for example is a single parent effectively being required to fulfil the roles of father and mother to two young boys. He is also the manager of the local branch of a bank. In addition he belongs to the Apex Club and is a keen sailor. So he clearly wears more than one hat and dips into more than one pond of contacts.

For most of us, each role probably involves a different set of contacts. The contacts you develop in any one sphere of activity tend to share similar values and interests. In other words, the "like"-talks-to-"like" principle discussed earlier is at work and this tends to go hand in hand with a passive (rather than a more directed) personal networking style, in many cases resulting in the individual having close-knit personal networks in each of the different spheres of activity.

Which types of links and aspects of your personal networks you wish to focus on will, of course, depend upon which particular spheres of activity you most want to succeed in. They will also depend on how those links might give you access to ponds that in turn give you access to still other ponds which give you access to opportunities and success in business, social areas, sports, politics or whatever. Contacts are of course sometimes overlapped across different spheres of activity, which has been the basis of so many soap operas, melodramas and farces – for example, social contact with the boss's wife, or mixes between politics and business contacts. Such instances of overlap can and should be explored in the development of contacts with others (see Chapter 5, "Ah-ha, It Is a Small World"), for it is the points of commonality – particularly other people whom you and I know in common – that form the basis of an evolving relationship between us.

The trick is to be able to marry personal networking with personal objectives. Assuming that you are clear about your objectives, take a good, hard look at your existing personal network in the most relevant spheres of activity. Which spheres, for purposes of gaining knowledge or advice and/or opportunities, are essential to realising your objectives (for example business, professional, sporting, church)? What links are not there that should be, and what links are there that should not be or that are really superfluous or even dangerous?

In Jeffrey Archer's best-selling novel *First Among Equals*, one of the major characters in the book, in spite of many tries, continually misses out on endorsement for a seat in parliament. The reason for this is that his "patron" is really his worst enemy and systematically undermines his chances of both financial and electoral success. It is only after several such experiences that one of the local political king-makers (who incidentally loathes this patron and also has more powerful connections in politics and business) tells the character what is really going on behind the scenes and helps him to break the nexus.

Perhaps you are holding onto a contact who prevents you from meeting others or who in some way undermines your chances of success. The tactics that you employ will sometimes involve making links with several people in just one sphere, and at other times with just one person but across several spheres. This latter approach could mean dropping a particular link if it cannot be broadened to encompass several spheres, or can only be broadened at high cost to you. Alternatively, perhaps for a particular contact one sphere can be dropped and another retained (for example drop the social aspects but retain the business dimensions) – sometimes a tricky operation!

Rebecca is a radio journalist. She has changed jobs a number of times, as journalists learning their trade invariably do. She has lived and worked in two small communities (about 40,000 people) and each time, because of the central part the radio station plays in the life of the community, she formed many work associations and friendships and the lines between these associations became blurred. So Rebecca found herself working and playing with many of the same people. They all became very close and when she left the rift was painfully felt by all.

Because she missed them so much she kept going back to visit. But eventually the demands associated with making new links in the new job and new communities became too much. However, the old links are still valued although some have disappeared and she keeps in touch with a number of them on a more or less regular basis. One of her former colleagues on the radio station is now a station manager in another town. While driving through that town recently she called to see him for about 10 minutes. A month later he asked her to do some freelance work for him (recorded voice-over commercials, which she also had to write). This was a lucrative little side source of income to her existing radio job and one that effectively spreads her influence and reputation across the industry. She is learning that strategic and directed networking pays!

Objectives

But Rebecca did not have a clear-cut objective that she then set about networking her way to achieve. Rather, she kept her old links alive and that led almost by accident to an additional opportunity that met her needs. Her personal network had been broadened across more than one pond and it was that diversity of linkage that led to the opportunity for some additional income. She did not start with the need, set an objective and then network her way to it.

If you start with a particular objective – after setting broader goals, thinking positively and doing most of the other things that "success" books say you should – then how do you go about networking your way to the achievement of that objective? How do you marry the two elements of success: objectives (part of "strategy") on the one hand, and personal networks (part of "structure") on the other hand?

A Case Study

The answer to this question is best illustrated by an actual case. You will perhaps recall Bill who capitalised upon his spare-time interest in horticulture (see Chapter 5, "Ah-ha, It Is a Small World"). He was the middle-aged manager who was in danger of being locked into his closely-knit little network, but who vastly broadened his linkages and opportunities at the same time as he turned his love of horticulture into a new business.

A major objective Bill had set himself was to gain publicity for his new business by hosting a weekly television program on gardening. He knew he could make a success of it if only he could find a sponsor for the program and a cooperative television station. Certain connections had to be made with others. Some of these would be key people who could make or break his chances of success, for they could directly influence whether the objective could be achieved or else they would add expertise in a particular way. These "influencers" or "sanctioners" are often integral to achievement of any successful outcome. They must, therefore, be identified and included in the tactics of networking to achieve objectives. Bill had identified one of the "influencers" as a likely commercial sponsor for his television program. He considered that a young entrepreneurial group would be most suited, in particular Fred Bates, the head of Bates Seeds, would be worth a try.

Only one of the major television stations did not currently broadcast a gardening program. Some years before Channel 6 had broadcast a gardening program, which was a flop. But Bill reckoned the time was now ripe for the channel to try again with the new format he had in mind. He discovered that the key decision maker on new programs at Channel 6 was the program director, Charlie Robson. So Bill made a mental note of him as a potential "influencer" or "sanctioner" as somebody he must network his way to if at all possible. Also at Channel 6 was Marietta Miles. She had a reputation of being a top producer, of being able to put a show together in a highly professional manner and of obtaining the most from her talent – another potential "influencer".

So what Bill was doing was establishing an objective and identifying three people who would most probably have a significant impact on his ability to achieve that objective – Bates of Bates Seeds, and Robson and Miles of Channel 6.

Diagrams

Being a good networker and conscious of the underlying structural relationships, Bill diagrammed the situation he was trying to manage (see Figure 8.1). Of his many contacts, several came to mind as people who might conceivably have linkage across to the "influencers" – Robson, Miles and Bates. Bill put these people on the diagram too – that is Nelson, Morgan, Jones, etcetera – and he pencilled in his reasons for considering each of them in this exercise (see Figure 8.1).

His direct contacts (Nelson, Morgan, Jones, etcetera) had cross-linkages between them that Bill knew about or suspected was the case. When he put in these cross-connections (Figure 8.1), a small pond emerged of horticulturally oriented people who were inter-connected with each other (Jones, Wright, Rose and Cooper). The cross-linkages in Bill's personal network also suggested opportunities for useful indirect contacts. For example, the fact that Rose was indirectly connected to Bates via both Cooper and Jones was taken advantage of by Bill much later when he decided to involve the Horticultural Society in his television program.

Having developed a picture of his own small set of contacts and how they were interrelated, Bill then looked for linkage across to the "influencers" or "sanctioners". Nelson, the contact in films, knew Miles and verified that she was definitely the best producer at Channel 6. However, Nelson did not know Robson, but believed that there was a good working relationship between Miles and Robson; so Bill pencilled in the Miles/Robson link.

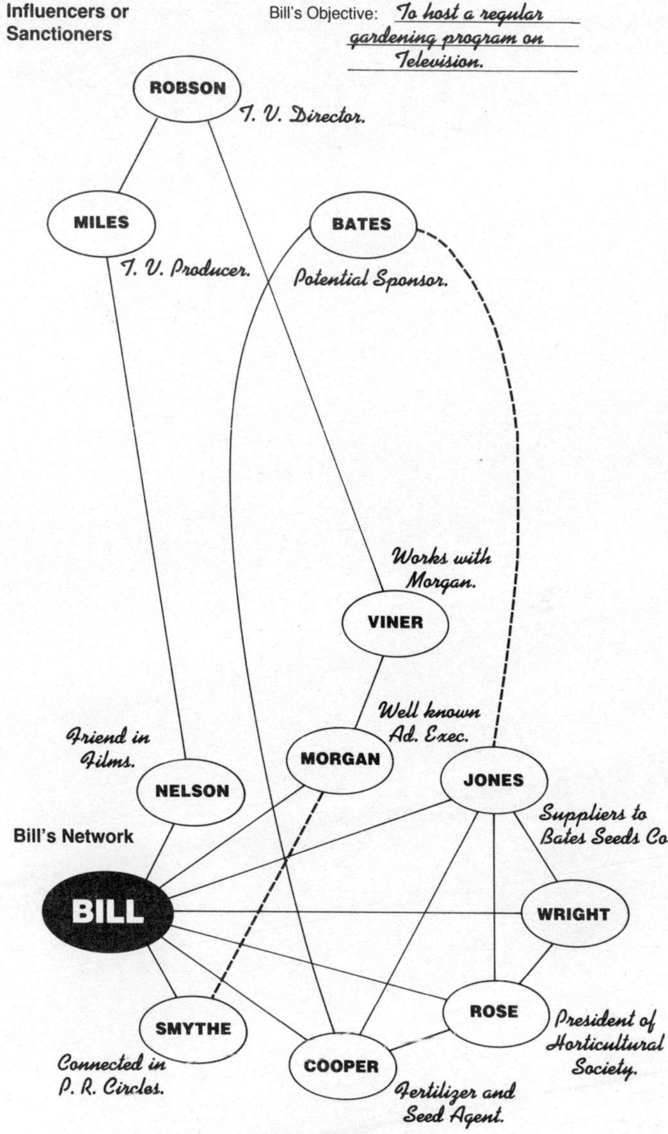

Figure 8.1
The key to Bill's success – marrying his network with his objective

Influencers or Sanctioners

Your Objective: ____________________

Your Network

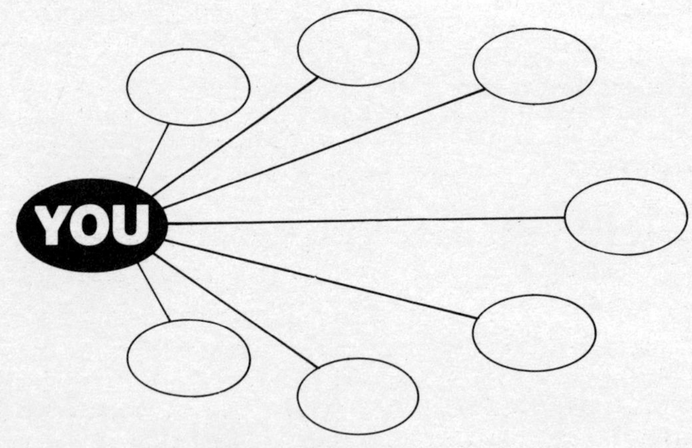

Figure 8.2

Two of Bill's direct contacts had effective relationships with the head of Bates Seeds – Cooper in particular, and Jones to a lesser extent (hence a dotted line from Jones to Bates). Both verified that in their opinion Bates Seeds would be a likely sponsor and a good firm for Bill to be associated with and to be seen to be associated with.

A connection was still needed to Robson. When he discovered that none of his own contacts had a direct link with Robson, Bill probed to see if there were any intermediary persons who could provide the indirect linkage that he needed across to Robson. In discussions with Bill's advertising executive friend Morgan, it turned out that a close colleague of Morgan's was Tony Viner who had an excellent working relationship with Robson. Bill then arranged an introduction to Viner who later put in a good word for him to Robson.

Strategic Success

A gardening program was established. The joy of having achieved this was enormously rewarding to Bill and it was itself highly successful. However, he concluded he would not have been successful if he had concentrated only on the psychological elements of success – the setting of goals, the developing of a positive self-image, positive attitudes and so on – or if he had concentrated only on the personal networking elements of success – broadening his contacts, jumping up to other ponds, moving to a crossroads position and so on. His personal networking was successful but it was strategically driven toward goal-achievement. The strategy dictated the structure, but neither could have really worked without the other.

Bill used his connections and developed them: firstly, to survey the situation, to verify that these were the right people and the key potential influencers or people whose sanction he would need to obtain if his objectives were to be met. Secondly, he used these links to lay the groundwork that he wanted but not to actually fire any shots. He was careful not to lose control of the situation by letting others try to sell his ideas for him, but he did use these contacts so that they paved the way for him to have access to the right people, and then for him to be regarded by them as a highly reputable and credible person. He thus extended himself through and with others in the direction he wanted to go, to achieve an objective that would have been difficult without them.

When he subsequently met each of the "influencers", they had heard favourable things about him and knew somebody whom he knew. Therefore, each had a person they could "share" in discussions with Bill to begin with – various points of commonality to refer to – which is a fundamental point in the development of effective relationships (see Chapter 5, Ah-Ha, It is a Small World"). Bill made the most of his discussions with them to network his way back in the opposite direction, that is, from the "influencers" towards Bill and his personal network. One thing he discovered in discussions with Robson was that Robson thought of himself as having reasonably green fingers. Furthermore, because Robson knew something of the plants in which Bill specialised, he knew one of the horticulturalists Bill knew well. As well, Robson had recently met Bill's advertising executive friend Morgan, via the intermediary contact Viner, and he spoke well of Morgan's professional achievements. A small world indeed, but sometimes it can be even smaller if you decide that that is the way you want it to be and you build up the points of commonality.

Bill was successful not only because he networked across from his own contacts to the key persons who could influence the achievement of his objective, but when he got there he also probed for linkages from their point of view back into his own particular world. He, in effect, simulated the feeling of a small world with the people with whom he wanted to establish relationships. He weaved his links across the appropriate persons and subgroups, keeping his objective in mind. And his objective was influenced by holding a positive mental attitude, positive self-image and so on – crucial steps for the achievement of success. But on top of that Bill's objective was influenced, indeed, was made possible, by his positive personal networking.

Figure 8.2 is a diagram of the type used by Bill. Of course it can be adapted to suit more or fewer people, but the concept that it illustrates is important – the horse with the cart, that is, the strategy (Where do you want to go?) with the structure (How are you going to get there?) – the two basic elements of success.

Checklist

Chapter 8

- Your strategies for life fulfilment will not and cannot work properly unless your personal networks are so structured that they allow you to get there.
- If you don't know where you are going, you are sure to end up somewhere else.
- Strategies and tactics must involve setting your objectives clearly and listing the ponds to which you want access, and then making the connections that enhance your achievement of the objective.
- This may mean: making new links, dropping others, dropping a link in one sphere or broadening it into other spheres.
- Networking in a deliberate fashion to meet an objective means: identifying key people who can influence the achievement of that objective, taking stock of your existing contacts, and networking your way across to those key people.
- Your personal network structures need to be adapted to "match" your strategies.

PART II

Chapter 9

Network Liberation in the Information Society

Develop a New Lease of Life – Make Connections that Give You the Freedom to Succeed

These are times of incredible change. Individuals have increased freedom of lifestyles and increased freedom of ways of acting and opportunities to succeed. Yet with all of this there are still subtle constraints operating for most of us that restrict freedom of movement and freedom to succeed. More subtle (too pervasive to permit recognition) and more powerful than government-level censorship is our own micro social censorship.

The point is that you and I are personal networkers, but consciously networking to achieve your goals, rather than just letting connections with others sort themselves out, will make a vast difference to your chances of being able to achieve your goals.

Do You Have the Freedom to Succeed?

The passive or socio-emotional approach to personal networking is where you let associations with others arise and develop around you with little conscious effort about the process—often on the ''like''-talks-to-''like'' basis. It is more comfortable and less challenging this way. At every turn of the corner contacts are determined by way of similar attitudes and similar interests, not by different attitudes and different sets of information and ideas. And yet it can only be the differences from where you are and what you know that can be usefully added to your current knowledge to allow you to achieve.

The passive style of personal networking feels good, helps with your own identity and helps to confirm what seems to be important to you, but it does not provide many different perspectives on problems or solutions. The net result of a passive style of networking is a socio-emotional, supportive type of personal network – the small pond, close-knit situation – which is stifling in terms of exposure to new ideas and opportunities that are now the stuff of success.

Phillip Hurst and one of the authors (Anne) both joined the staff of the Riverina College of Advanced Education back in 1970 when it was nominated as one of the new genre educational establishments, a college of advanced education. On one of Phillip's recent visits to Australia, we were reminiscing about the paths both of us had travelled since those days together in Wagga. At the time we both left the college, job opportunities abounded for people like us. We both took those opportunities. Phillip went to America with little money and few contacts and did a master's degree in law at the University of Virginia. From there he was offered a position in a New York firm of attorneys and from there went to the World Bank. He has now taken a very well-paid job in London as legal counsel at Morgan Guarantee Bank – one of the largest merchant banks in the world.

However, many of our original colleagues are still on the staff at the college. They have as much, maybe more talent than we have. Some of them would, we believe, want to step out and expand, but the job market is such, and they have now stayed so long and are so comfortable, that they say it is too difficult for them to take such a step.

More recently, Tony Palumbo, one of Anne's other colleagues at the same college, has become one of the few therapeutic puppeteers in the world and now visits Australia conducting seminars as a visiting specialist. He has studied in the United States, France and Italy. His worldwide network in

RESCUE
CONTACTS
SMALL POND
KNIGHT

the puppeteer fraternity is second to none. He has married his psychology qualifications to the therapeutic application of psycho-drama, and has thus created a unique and valuable link between two professions, which is bringing him considerable success. But it took him a lot longer than Phillip or myself to find the courage to step out of his comfortable Wagga niche and do what his heart told him he should do. Nevertheless he has done it and the results have been worth all the worry and anguish he has experienced along the way.

Decide, Don't Abdicate the Choice to Succeed

If you are a big fish in a small pond and continue to live in it, what you are doing in effect is abdicating the freedom to choose, abdicating that responsibility from you to the group, the members of your personal network. The group decides what is admissible and what is not, what is appropriate and what is not. This doesn't usually happen in an overtly determined way but, as part of the way that groups work. As we've mentioned before, the essence of keeping membership, of continuing to be a big fish in a small pond, is to share viewpoints, to see things in the same or similar ways in order to keep the ties and share the socio-emotional rewards of commonality, friendship and support.

All of which is to say that a price is paid for continuing to live in a close-knit personal network and that this needs to be fully recognised. For the support and comfort that is afforded from the small pond, one must give up an amount of personal freedom to the group – to decide collectively what ideas and viewpoints are appropriate and, therefore, the opportunities that you can know about and you can act upon. You may decide that the wisest course of action is to visit the small pond, to use it as a base, but to be aware of the costs inherent if you make the decision to reside there permanently and exclusively.

When you hitch your wagon to a close-knit group, opportunities to achieve become constrained to the (usually) limited set of contacts of contacts that any group as a whole has.

Therefore, if the principle is accepted that the achievement of goals not only depends upon the self but upon others, and if there is a very limited range of others because your contacts are mostly in touch with each other anyway, then the freedom to choose and succeed is constrained by the group. This is a deceptive entrapment because it feels so comfortable and so supportive and you may not know it has even happened until perhaps it's too late. Have you examined your situation recently?

Develop a More Commanding Personality

Commonsense suggests that people with outgoing personalities will mix with a broader range of people and, therefore, develop rather more diverse, open-knit or "distributed" types of personal networks. In other words, personality factors have an influence upon the types of personal networks that people evolve.

From his earliest years Malcolm was a reader and a scholar. He grew up in a small town on the Queensland border. One of the authors (Anne) came to know of him because of his lucid writing and the quality of his thought as a university professor. A friend once said that he went to school with him and he was always categorised as a misfit – a fish, if you will, out of water. He was the butt of jokes and no girl wanted to dance with him. His intellectual leanings destined him for an academic career and he escaped the small town labels, flourishing and growing in the wide pond, where he was very much a fish in water of a much bigger dimension. Now his old schoolfriends are proud to boast that they once knew him as a schoolboy. It makes you wonder what his life would have been like without that escape and what kind of person he would have been allowed to become.

Obviously there is much validity for the commonsense view stated earlier that personality factors will have an influence upon the type of personal network that somebody evolves. But as Malcolm's case illustrates, the argument can also be turned around. People can and do develop more vital and commanding personalities as an outcome of their networking efforts. Because they are no longer locked into close-knit personal networks or because they are no longer locked out of them, their outlook on life is altered. They seem brighter and more confident in their approach to problems and in dealing with situations. Personal networking to achieve one's goals allows a person to grow – like taking the brakes off on a car pointed downhill – and it also can be an incredibly positive and energising factor.

Tony's confidence has increased following his work with puppets and his confidence and view of himself has also been enormously enhanced. Phillip has visibly grown. Sometimes it is three years between meetings for us and so the difference is noticed. He is more and more interesting and exciting to be with and his knowledge, wisdom and view of the world have expanded beyond anything either of us could have imagined back in 1970. Malcolm has been released from the prison of the small pond and, of course, it is easy to see what a "prison" it could have become for him.

When times are changing, as the song goes, the natural inclination for individuals and, indeed, organisations is to batten down the hatches until the storm abates. What people who take that decision might one day wake to find is that they have, in effect, taken a decision not to participate in the excitement and opportunities of the new era and that by doing so they have lost the initiative. For, as the saying goes, not to decide is to decide.

Network Liberation in the Information Society

A few short years ago it would not have been possible to make the assertion with any degree of honesty that opportunities are open to everyone. Most people were locked into communities and well defined-roles within them with little prospect of change. Cinderella's rise from scullery maid to princess was a 500 million to one chance. That is why it was called a fairy story. But with the advent of the car and the telephone and now with computers and satellite communications, the organisation of society has changed dramatically.

In Barry Jones's book *Sleepers Wake* he exhorts Australia to wake to the dramatic implications of the information revolution, 20 years after Alvin Toffler blew the whistle in *Future Shock*. Since both these books were written the process of change has grown exponentially and the connections between information and networking have become more and more obvious. It is exactly this connection that Naisbitt points up by coining the phrase "high tech high touch" in *Megatrends* – the connection between technology, information and people.

Whether we choose to call it the "third-wave era" or the information society, our present economy is based on the value of information, and the technologies that store and process that information. In turn this change has also led to a reassessment of the role and value of people.

Because this dramatic change is happening now and is happening quickly, there is little time for people to adjust to it over a long period. And because the change is so "on top of us", we often don't have that distant perspective to see the full extent of its challenges and its opportunities. That is why many people are still locked into an industrial age mentality (or "mindset") while the information age calls for a whole new set of behaviours, understandings and relationships. What we need is what Kuhn, in *The Study of Scientific Revolutions* calls a "paradigm shift" or what Hilmer, in *When the Luck Runs Out* calls a change in mindsets.

Cutting and Honing of Information

Jenny, for example, in spite of her skinny frame and freckled face was hired as a sales assistant only because she insisted on it. Her boss was taken with her enthusiasm but not her good looks! But he soon realised he had struck gold. Jenny had a computerised memory for customers' names, faces and the things they liked and needed. "Remember that French lace you couldn't get last month, Mrs Collins," the boss heard her say one day, "well, we have got it in now. Is it too late for that dress you wanted to trim?" She remembered the size of Mr Mervyn's pipes although he himself had forgotten it. She knew everyone's dress and shirt size and what they liked; what they gave Aunt Flo for her birthday last year; that there was a wedding or engagement or birth coming up. She sent cards to customers and let them know about new stock they might need to suit whatever occasion. Jenny left to go on the payroll of one of the biggest retailers in America as a trainee buyer. Her boss made the mistake of bragging about her talents to a visiting retailer and, much to his chagrin, his network secured her the new job.

But the lesson was not lost on Jenny. She realised she had a rare informational talent. Small-town girl and freckles or no freckles, she is now one of the most valued retail resources in the country and she systematically uses her talents to her own and everyone else's advantage. Jenny's system of customer preference and needs is now part of a well-organised computerised information system that she herself designed. She knew how it should work because she already had it in her head. It was primarily based on a good memory but, more importantly, also on a real interest and affection for people.

Her success illustrates that it is people who ultimately process information – cutting, honing, crafting it into knowledge, and giving it meaning, producing the usable output of the information process. In some circles this usable output is called "intellectual property", having all the value but few of the attributes of capital assets, the basis of the old industrial society.

If you ask any group of people at random where the primary source of their information comes from, they will almost always answer that it is through other people.

Circulation of Information

It is people who generate and develop ideas. Ideas then lead to activity and some of this activity will involve sharing the idea and developing it to another stage. All technology has done is speed up the process of transference and allow it to be much more generally accessed. So you and I, Jim, Mary, Dan and Sheila generate the raw material of new developments to add value to it. We offer services associated with it and we keep the process in circulation.

If you see information in this way you will notice that it only has value if it *is* in circulation. Like money, it has to change hands and be in circulation to, at worst, maintain its value, or at best, to grow and multiply in value. Communications technology – the movement of people, ideas and information around the globe – is making it more and more difficult for special groups to hide their secrets and to hoard their power, even if they were stupid enough to think they could do that for long.

Scarcity and Abundance

Networking, then, in the information age, is based on an open perspective and on reciprocity and access, as well as on the idea of abundance not scarcity. The notion of scarcity was developed by people who saw the oil or the coal or the forests and recognised that there was a finite and limited supply of such raw material. What the universe – the atom and modern physics – has taught us is that the universe is abundant. As Buckminster Fuller points out, it is only limited by the limitations of our own thinking, knowledge and information.

The concept of scarcity so beloved of the economists, loses currency in the face of the information economy. Information is a very different commodity that does not readily fit the supply and demand model of economics. Information is not finite. Unlike other commodities, when you give information you still have it, and if you are discriminating in who you share it with, you finish with more than you started with. There are abundant opportunities and ideas available through contact with others. That knowledge can be held by any number of people at any place in society and its value is very much related to the needs of time and place.

A company, for example, might spend millions on research to solve a problem when the best knowledge and information is in the heads of the people they employ at the coalface. The solution might be relatively cheaply obtained just by seeking inputs from those people. The receptionist who fields a call from an angry customer could hold the key to a fall-off in sales. But is she or he ever asked? If a company that does not provide a means to reticulate information around and across its organisation is missing out on its most valuable resource and, incidentally, is not using its people effectively. However, such sharing has to be rewarded and this is where reciprocity comes in.

Reciprocity

If I share information with you and you use it against me, or you don't reciprocate at some time in a way that shows you value what I have given you, then it is unlikely I will share anything with you again. I might even pass on to others that you can not be trusted.

If I take your idea and claim it as my own or sell it to a competitor, or if I do not involve you in the decisions that flow from it or give you credit for the original idea, even though it might have changed somewhat, I will suffer the same fate.

If I help you and you never help either me or any of my friends or family... well you get the idea by now. This kind of reciprocity didn't matter when information wasn't as valuable as it is now. It does matter in a society where information has become a very valuable resource indeed. Ah, but we can hear you saying, what about competition? Do you really expect us to believe that we should share what we are and what we know with all and sundry?

No, of course not. But what you must recognise is that you will only have exclusive use to the raw material of information for a short time. For it to grow in value, as we have said before, it must be shared. Strategically you have to decide who you share that information with. You will probably also have to work in a team to bring an idea to fruition because an idea is only as good as its application. You will need people to help you apply what you know and they will have various skills – market experts, publicists, financiers. If you are looking for a job you will need people who will open doors for you, you will need to tell your employer what you know and you may even need to demonstrate this in some way. If it is a red-hot new invention you may only have the leading edge for 12 months. After that you will need to work on staying ahead of the competition or working on a new invention or application of the original idea.

So the more contacts you have, the more strategically placed and reciprocal they are – the more crossroads-type personal network you have – the more you are likely to have a broad choice of multidisciplinary friends and experts who can help you with that process. Of course you *also* need to know who you can trust. Your networks will be the best informants about who is trustworthy and who is not.

Coping with Information

Most of us suffer in the information society from information overload. There is so much of it around that one can only say the world is now in danger of suffering from information pollution. Strategies for success will depend on getting the right information at the right time.

The traditional approach to handling information was to learn it. This is often no longer viable – it is just not possible for you to learn everything that is likely to be relevant to your needs. Time spent trying to soak up all the relevant knowledge is time spent not putting the knowledge into practice. Besides, absolute truths yesterday are not absolute truths today. As information expands, so does our knowledge. Still more important, however, is that it is simply not possible to store every morsel of information in your head. There's too much of it, it cannot be done.

Links "on Line"

What has to be done is to access information and advice when it is wanted, the very best information at the right time. Which means that the links necessary for your success have to be established or, in computer jargon, be "on line". Links to the people who do or can influence decisions or who can provide you with the information, advice or opportunities that you need, when you need them, have to be readily available.

Thus we are emphasising the strategic retrieval through your network of relevant bits of information, not the learning individually of everything that could conceivably influence your chances of success. Your personal networking must help you to have "on-line" contacts and therefore access through them to their contacts and worlds of knowledge you need when you need it.

You must also develop a flexible and open approach to new ideas and a capacity to use both your left and right sides of the brain, to think, as De Bono would say, laterally. This means thinking wholistically as well as in a linear fashion – seeing the totality and not just the immediate details. This is a very different mindset from that of educational theorists of the past, which many present pundits would have us return to in the present.

In the next section we explore the dynamics of the old boy network, and the difference between that perspective of networking and the new imperatives of the information society. Understanding the differences between locked-in systems, like the old boy network, and more open network structures can be an important key to your success.

Checklist

Chapter 9

- More subtle and more powerful than any government-level censorship is our own microsocial censorship.
- The passive styles of networking of the past (rather than the more strategic styles of the future) led to small-pond situations. However in the years ahead this will not fit the needs of the information society where success will depend upon new ideas and new opportunities.
- Networking in the information society is based on abundance not scarcity, and an abundance of ideas becomes available through contact with others.
- Organisations that don't use the information and knowledge of their own people can be missing out on a mine of information.
- Reciprocity in sharing information is the name of the game. Give and you shall receive.
- For information to grow in value it must be shared. Like money it must be in circulation.
- The right information at the right time means strategic retrieval of information is more important to the individual than the ability to store it.

Chapter 10
The Old Boy Network
Beware – Certain Ponds Are Probably Stagnant

In the information era nobody can rely on the old boy network, whether to keep them safe from exposure or to maintain exclusive power. Discussions that include networking will often get a response that links it with the old boy network (or OBN). This phrase was originally coined to describe that fraternity of alumnae of the English public schools that operated for centuries to serve the interests of the British upper class. We might go so far as to say that the old boy network has given networking a bad name! This is because the old boy network operated in the past as a means of locking up power and information, just as Alexander the Great did centuries ago. (see Chapter 6, "The Psychology of the Small Pond").

Such tight-knit, little enclaves still exist, of course. An article in the *Australian Financial Review* on Patrice Marriott, Elders IXL's most senior woman executive, who has been stationed in London, illustrates this point:

> *I had travelled to and from London (on scholarships) since I was 18. I had the impression that because women had been prominent in British social and political life, it would be easy for a woman there. But the Allied case illustrated what a tight little club the City is. There aren't any women members of the club. There is an initial curiosity and patronisation. It took me a while to learn how to deal with that.*
>
> *In the early days it was exceptionally lonely. London so-*

ciety is hard to penetrate. In May I received my first at-home invitation for Sunday lunch. I thought, right, I'm on a different social network now. (Australian Financial Review, *5 December, 1986, p.16).*

It is not surprising that Patrice Marriott experienced this exclusion since Britain is, after all, the home of the old boy network. The implications of this system and how it successfully locked up information and access to power are wonderfully and comprehensively discussed in a publication called *Networks! – Who We Know and How We Use Them* by Tim Heald. In this book Heald describes how the upper class in Britain were schooled from an early age in the rites and mores of its culture, which encompassed education at certain schools and universities. Dress, speech, manners, myths, legends and history are all part of the maintenance of the British upper-class culture within which the OBN thrived and to some extent still does.

This culture made possible the accumulation and maintenance of power, wealth and government to generation after generation of the British upper class. It was accessed eventually but slowly by the new rich of the industrial revolution who bought peerages for themselves, places at the great schools, and husbands and wives for their children from the ranks of impoverished aristocrats – thus becoming neatly integrated into the OBN system at the same time as breathing new life into it.

The old boy network system of power (a closed network if ever there were one) also made possible the conspiracy between Guy Burgess, Donald Maclean, Kim Philby and Anthony Blunt, who provided information from within the safety of the British secret service to the USSR. All undergraduates together at Cambridge during the 1930's, these four men had a strong philosophic belief in a common ideal (paradoxically totally opposed to the British class structure) developed during their student days, as well as a strong and secret bond to one another (they were all homosexual) nurtured by the OBN system. This bond was further facilitated

It's an attack from some outsiders.... form the Bentleys into a circle
Old Boys Network
Old Boys
Old Boys Network
Old Boys
KNIGHT

and maintained largely by virtue of another secret system, MI5, within the British secret service.

Scandals like the Burgess, Maclean, Philby and Blunt incidents, and others involving the CIA and politicians and bureaucrats who use and exploit the closed system to do everything from winning elections (Watergate), hiding faults in the space program (Challenger) or selling arms to Iran (Irangate), illustrate the dangers of such systems and the widespread suspicion in which they are now held. The information revolution and the power of electronic media, of course, now make it harder to keep such secrets secret for too long.

But it is not just the upper echelons of society with their immediate access to power and money that has operated on the basis of a closed power network. The close association of certain sections of police forces all over the world with the Mafia, politicians, drug runners and other criminal groups has been, and still is, one of the hardest nuts for honest communities to crack. New South Wales power-brokers have now also fallen foul of the technological revolution. Electronic devices used to tape and tap have recently been the undoing of politicians and judges as well as public servants and private citizens.

Secrecy is the essence of such old boy connections and secrecy is becoming harder to rely on and maintain. In Australia in 1980 Frank Costigan used technology to trace the flow of money to find the guilty parties in tax evasion and, in addition, discovered hitherto unsuspected chicanery. When the politicians didn't want to know, the media blew the whistle on what Costigan knew. Richard Nixon used the tools of the information society but was caught out by the realities of the information society – a clash that would not have been possible in a previous era. Geoff Kennett and Andrew Peacock both would, no doubt, bear witness to the public nature of modern communications technology.

Everyone potentially has access to what the power brokers know. And because of this the game and its rules have now dramatically changed. This change also has another side to it. The process of locking in also ensures a process of locking out. Look around at the trouble many of our Australian institutions are in as a result. Look at the British economy of not so long ago and ask whether there was a connection between the old boy network and Britain's economic decline. Look particularly at the implications the information society has for politicians and for the style of politics in the future.

Information-based Politics

John Hatton, a politician of independent persuasion, came to power because he understood the importance of the issues of the day in his own electorate. He successfully plugged local issues but linked them to more global concerns. Because he kept his ear to the ground and was prepared to speak fairly openly on issues of importance that no other group would touch, he ensured his continuing place in parliament since his own electorate viewed him as a kind of independent hero. His success could also largely be attributed to a capacity to follow up leads, respond to people who wanted to keep him informed and the confidence that he could be trusted with that information.

From a little-known local politician with no hope of a Cabinet posting (since he is outside all political parties), he nevertheless has carved out a significant and successful role for himself in the life of the State of New South Wales. He never forgot that staying in touch through diverse types of networks is the key to understanding what the major future concerns will be. A small issue now might be a big one tomorrow, but you will never know how to judge that unless you stay in touch with the source of information – networks at the local and grassroots level.

Politicians are by inclination excellent networkers. That's how they're elected in the first place. Unless they come from the Tammany Hall variety, that historical place and series of events which have become synonomous with closed shop political dirty tricks, their stock-in-trade is "how to win friends and influence people". But like most other fields of endeavour, politics is also changing in the face of the capacity of people to be better informed and the development of a more diverse society. Nixon relied, as we have mentioned before, on the tools of trade of the information society. At the same time he failed to observe that in the information society it has become virtually impossible to keep guilty secrets secret. Because we are now into the era of open systems and access to information, the old boy network, whatever form that happens to take, is not the way to go.

By all means, have contacts in as many OBNs as are possible or relevant, but do not let yourself get locked into one. Recognise the dangers of ponds that become stagnant and lock out the source of fresh and sparkling water, which brings new life and new vitality.

It is now not only possible but also probable that groups of like-minded people will share information across continents and even across the globe. The black power movement, the women's movement, the conservation movement, the pressure from disabled people for independent living and deinstitutionalisation, the grey power movement, and the peace movement are all outcomes of this communications process, as much as the ability of banks, financiers and stock exchanges to trade and syndicate deals and move money across the globe at a moment's notice.

Politicians should know all this but the problem is that, once elected, they often lose touch with what is going on outside their own closed network of colleagues, minders and other hangers-on. At a time when these networks should be broadening, the net actually tightens and constrains their vision and the possibility of movement. They run the risk of losing touch with what is happening around them, preferring to cling tenaciously or just out of ignorance to a group of outdated ideologies or beliefs about the world. Ponds that get cut off become stagnant and the fish usually end up dead!

In Chapter 6, "The Psychology of the Small Pond", we discussed the dangers associated with the locked-in quality of much of our senior management. A similar problem exists with trade unions whose tendency is to view the world exclusively through the eyes of their closed enclave. At best they widen their contacts to the industrial relations club, but that, too, is a closed coterie of people who gain their living and their identity from working within an industry that is essentially devoted to maintaining a legalised system of confrontation.

But the implications of the failure of all these groups to observe the signs of change, although of enormous significance, are less instantly dramatic or publicly exposed. Witness the sight of Malcolm Fraser who, on losing the federal election in 1983, wept openly on national television.

Openness

Open networking processes are also poorly understood by people in power because political power operates on exactly the reverse precepts and values: cornering the market on power. The open networking concept, as we have mentioned before, works on the basis of power as an unlimited resource not on scarcity, but on abundance.

The Australian Democrats believe they have solved this problem by instituting regular ballots on issues amongst their membership. This reflects a continuing sensitivity to a diversity of opinions and wider networks, as well as an ability to move with the times. How long this will last, of course, is very much a matter for speculation.

So what do the Bob Hawkes or John Howards do about their position? How can they keep in touch with what is going on and still handle the enormous workloads involved with being in government. One of the ways, of course, is to look at the differences between being in government and in opposition. Opposition members are more open and have more time to listen to the unofficial version of what's happening, partly because they are hungry for information of any kind and therefore receptive. Some, however, like the arch-conservatives or arch-radicals, are not interested in anything other than information that reflects their own ideological position. But we are putting them to one side in this debate because we believe they will suffer the same fate as those who close themselves in once they gain political power.

Replicating the openness of opposition while in government means realising the dangers involved with a closed position and making opportunities to make it otherwise. Take the minister we know who has a panel of about 20 contacts and friends across a broad spectrum of society and whom he rings for their opinion about various matters when he wants another perspective. He doesn't ring them often or all at once. Each would receive about three calls a year, in addition to other reasons for contact he might have with them through social or business associations. After 20 years in politics he swears that this approach, together with a sensitivity to the problems that come to the door of his electoral office, keep him constantly updated.

Take John Button, for example, a minister who seeks to be in touch with issues and what is likely to change. He goes to a mixture of prestigious and less prestigious functions to get the feel of how people are thinking, and he tries not to rush away immediately after the speeches so he can talk about what is on people's minds. His secret is his genuine openness to criticism and to new ideas. He does not pull the blind down or seek gratification for his own ego.

One minister we know never welcomed bad news. He'd ask his staff what they thought, and after the first honest exchange the staff learned to keep their opinions to themselves. The penalty for speaking up was to be forced to listen to a tirade of why the minister was right and the rest of the world was wrong.

When Bob Hawke came to power he took a number of Premier Neville Wran's stabf to Canberra, hoping to replicate the political success kf one of the most outstandijgly electorally successful premierships in history. In retrospect, although some of their advice might have been very good indeed, the

New South Wales style of cynical, ad hoc, knock-'em-down power politics did not transfer well to Canberra where the challenge is different. Hawke lost touch around the middle of 1985 and failed to do anything about it until the end of 1986. By that time he had locked himself into many positions from which it was difficult to escape. Not the least of Hawke's problems arose because of a tendency to believe his own publicity – a nice safe cocoon – a tendency, of course, that must be counteracted by being exposed to criticism (harsh and otherwise) and being forced to deal with it.

Similarly, New South Wales Premier, Barrie Unsworth, went within 54 votes of being cast into political oblivion by being insensitive to his Rockdale, Sydney, electorate, which was to provide him with entry to the Lower House. At first he said he would not live in Rockdale, then he bought a unit there but continued to live on the Upper North Shore. It seems he was not in touch either through his own ineffective networking or by merely receiving advice from those who wished to please him – shades of "Yes, Minister" – or both. He and they had both failed to read the signs of changing political behaviour and expectations in the electorate.

God knows where Malcolm Fraser's advisors were when he decided to call an election at the beginning of 1983, but he certainly wasn't listening to them if they were about. Perhaps it was another case of a man who thought he knew better than anyone else.

Phillip Adams is fond of telling the story of the time when his advertising agency was commissioned to carry out background research into the approach to be taken in the Advance Australia Campaign. The research results did not fit the prime minister's preconceptions and from Phillip Lynch down, no-one was prepared to break the news to Fraser. In the end Adams himself fronted up. "That's not what people tell me," said Fraser when confronted with the research results. "With respect, Prime Minister, our interviewees don't drink at the Melbourne Club," came Adam's now-famous reply. Fraser was locked into a mindset that, as it turned out, proved to be his undoing and, incidentally, the undoing of the Advance Australia Campaign – a campaign that, in retrospect turned out to be remembered more for its forgettable qualities than for anything else.

Checklist

Chapter 10

- The old boy network denotes a closed system of relationships but technology has made the closed system almost impossible to maintain for any length of time.
- The process of locking in information also robs the inside circle of important and necessary information on the outside. Hence the OBN can all too readily become a stagnant pond with mainly old ideas floating about plus sometimes one or two smelly fish.
- The stock in trade of politicians is how to win friends and influence people. They are by inclination excellent networkers.
- However, the tendency of many politicians is to lose touch with the grassroots. They get locked into close-knit and very supportive little networks that can be quite seductive but at the same time locks them out of other opportunities.
- Issue networks can make small issues big issues overnight, causing closed-in systems to be caught short.
- A crossroads style of personal networking, although not necessarily providing much comfort, is clearly preferable to a small (stagnant) pond for politicians to keep in touch.

Chapter 11

Seeking Success in Personal Networking

Using Networking if you are...

Mining the gold of our own and our friends' experiences has yielded up a rich harvest of inclusions for this book. Chapters 1 to 10 are studded with examples and they are there to illustrate the major arguments in favour of the "success thesis" we want you to take away with you. These experiences cover: women who have successfully networked into male-dominated environments; people who have used networking to get themselves out of difficulties; to act as brokers between groups; to pull themselves up by their bootstraps; to ensure themselves an interesting and productive old age; to develop a political style in tune with the times; and many more. Practice makes perfect, of course, and it is only when you start to apply what you know that you will yourself strike the gold that's out there waiting to be mined.

In this chapter and in Chapter 12 we outline a number of interesting personal networking experiences. The cases are typical of the challenges faced by people in a world in transition and are especially relevant if you are any of the following:

A. Climbing the corporate ladder
B. A chief executive
C. Looking for your first job
D. A community worker
E. A small business person
F. An entrepreneur

A. *Climbing the Corporate Ladder*

For better or worse over the time during which our large organisations have evolved to their present state, they have tended to take on a sameness that may have worked for the era in which they evolved, but that now makes them dysfunctional for the challenges of the information society.

They are dysfunctional largely because the way in which they are structured ensures that decisions will be slow, risks minimised or, more often still, no decision taken at all. But getting the right information, developing new ideas and adaptations are the lifeblood of our present period and the capacity to move fast when a good idea is "hot" is paramount to an organisation's success.

Many new ideas are generated at the bottom of an organisation, off to one side or in the middle. By the time they make their way up through several clearing houses, they have become more and more remote from the source from which they spring. They thus lose power and energy, or worse still, are seen as threats to the maintenance of certain people's jobs or the status quo that these people mistakenly feel the structure is set up to maintain. The chief executive or board would normally never know what they have lost through this process. But slowly and reluctantly there is a growing realisation that this process costs. Changes must be made because the rusty old machines are daily confronted by sleeker and leaner companies sprinting past them in the corporate race.

As for the public sector, the community expects something different in the future. The demand is for a new and more responsive approach from bureaucracies. The old systems are clearly out of date. Throwing money at them will not make them more efficient. New partnerships need to be forged; new linkages developed between ponds. The cultural gaps between private and public sectors need to be bridged since each has a great deal to learn from the other.

Diversity – the name of the game

Alvin Toffler's scenario in the *Third Wave* of a radically different kind of society in which "diversity, not standardisation is the order of the day – in which the mass is demassified and also rapidly changing" sums up the major challenge ahead for large organisations. The information age challenges organisations to deal with that complexity and diversity in a very new way.

Networks and networking are integral to that new way, and one of networking's greatest strengths is that it loosens up large bureaucratic organisations and helps them to become more adaptive and faster moving. It also requires a change in attitude, new processes, management and style. It can also bring about results even when it isn't encouraged but works well for the individual within the organisation, once he or she knows how to use it effectively. In her book *The Change Masters*, Rosabeth Moss Kanter found that people who had been with an organisation a long time, had spent some time working in different sections of it and used these connections to develop team support for innovation and change were the most effective innovators.

But people who are clever enough to know how to network throughout an organisation need not wait a long time. They can truncate the process by identifying key people with whom they have a common bond or purpose and get on with the business of building informal contacts and trust with them, on a project-by-project basis.

No matter how many lines of communication are drawn on formal organisational charts, attempts to depict the way things are supposed to work rarely, if ever, reflect the reality. Much of the real business both inside and outside organisations goes on in and out of the organisations' networks. Organisations by and large operate not on the basis of formal lines of communication, which tend to stifle creative exchange, but on the basis of a complex web of interlocking relationships and communications that until very recently remained a mystery to most people who work within them (apart for the most astute networkers). But it is now possible, on the basis of a set of concepts and computer software developed over 15 years by one of the authors (John), to chart these communication pathways in an easy-to-read graphical form.

These charts are called Netmaps. "Actual", "ought-to-be" and "what if" situations can be compared and action steps taken. And, as with personal networking, the "real" organisational networks can be examined in terms of how they either prevent strategies from working properly (for example, bottlenecks or lack of cohesion) or else facilitate them (for example, key people in key positions in the networks). Structure and strategy need to go hand in hand to maximise organisational performance, as well as personal performance. Every organisation operates on the basis of a particular culture. Throughout this book we have continually mentioned the importance of cultural networking, and in the chapter "Culturals Within Cultures" the matter is discussed in greater depth.

Cohesive organisations have a strong and unifying sense of purpose, good morale and communications, and a strong culture. Organisations in trouble are characterised by bad morale, undue circulation of rumours, discontent and a feeling of powerlessness among staff. They tend not to attract or hold good people. Excellent cultures are also more likely to enjoy strong and responsive leadership at all levels and to foster a relatively democratic and open environment – the essence of a networking environment. An environment, in other words, that releases the potential of its people to give of their best, to use and process information, both for their own and the organisation's benefit.

A few years ago the average executive had little notion of what the word culture meant outside a trip to the ballet or opera. Now some even declare that they want one by Monday, because the word is out that good corporate culture is one of the key factors in a successful business! But it is also a most complex factor.

Using a Lift

Jane is an MBA graduate with a degree in economics and experience in the banking field. Following her recruitment on campus by a large bank, she was posted to their head office in Sydney where she knew very few people. The bank had a reputation for being male dominated and she took the job there simply because it offered the best basic early training for a youngish MBA graduate entering the field. She didn't intend to stay more than two years knowing that the culture was not noted for its propensity to advance women into senior positions.

A lucky break came during her first six months at the bank. She found herself stuck in the lift with the new managing director for two hours! This opportunity might have been lost if Jane had not used the opportunity to answer the managing director's (we'll call him Frank) questions with honesty, frankness and intelligence. He, too, was looking for a chance to see the bank through the eyes of a newcomer and find out what was really going on down the line. So they traded secrets. Subsequently he became Jane's mentor.

Jane was moved to Frank's office as his executive assistant, and in due course he sent her out with a number of special assignment teams that were reviewing the bank's operations. She made contacts with a variety of staff across a range of departments and with a number of important clients. Jane's network and knowledge of the company grew, and because she was both bright and diplomatic she gained the trust of people at the operational level who saw her access to Frank as a way to make long-overdue changes within the company. In due course Frank knew who the frustrated movers and shakers were, mostly at first through Jane's network but then later through building on that network and expanding it in size and quality himself.

It was never actually spelled out that way, but Jane was also able to draw an accurate map of the corporate culture. Without that knowledge the changes that were finally made would not have been made as quickly, sensitively or effectively.

But Jane's success was really built on a number of other factors. The first thing she did correctly was to make the most of the first opportunity and contact. The second opportunity for success came by being involved in change-related activity where information was the key. The assignments were demanding, real and important to the company. The third important factor was the opportunities provided by assignments outside the organisation that allowed her to talk to people while travelling on planes or over meals. These opportunities don't come as easily in the day-to-day office environment. The fourth factor was trust – Jane was young and had little obvious power herself, except through her access to Frank. She did not, therefore, constitute a competitive threat but an information opportunity and she also proved trustworthy. The final factor, for Jane, was her interpersonal communications skills. She was sensitive, observant and a good listener, so she was given much more information than senior male executives would ever have been given under similar circumstances.

All of the above factors served Jane well in the bank's conservative, woman-shy organisational culture. In another culture at another time she may have had to be more aggressive but she adapted to the environment in which she found herself. The organisational restructure planned by the managing director took nearly five years to bring about completely but the early change strategies were based on many of Jane's observations and contacts, and Frank and others used that information to accelerate the process. Jane was part of his total change strategy and knowing this she met the challenge magnificently.

Now seven years later she herself has risen in the bank to become a divisional manager, and many of the important innovators identified during her first three years are now in senior positions and have been built into a cohesive network. More women are employed and that has also subtly changed the culture. Jane has been careful to network these women into a supportive group. This experience is not, of course, typical. After all, most people can't rely on the chance of a forced encounter with the managing director and some would not know how to take advantage of it anyway. But it does demonstrate the value of seizing opportunities, whatever they might be, when presented, and the power of networking for success.

B. The Chief Executive

No chief executive can afford to put complete trust in his or her formal management structure, hiding behind the facade of high office and hoping for the best. They have to get out there and find out what's really going on and much of that will be achieved through networks and networking. In Jane's case a new chief executive developed a network of contacts among the most innovative and get-up-and-go staff.

New chief executives are always at a serious disadvantage. They inherit a past culture, myths, values, attitudes and legends, as well as closed networks and established practices that they were not part of, and about which they cannot hope to gain knowledge unless they actually make it happen. At the top of the organisation they are in danger of being isolated from the real life of the organisation and knowledge of what goes on there and why things are done in certain ways.

Turning on the light

One company we know changed their chief executive four times in as many years. By the time Jim came on the scene the staff were so adept at keeping their leader in the dark (on the basis that he wasn't going to be there long anyway) that it took a long time to break through their wall of noncommunication. The company manufactured lighting equipment and was losing money when it shouldn't have been, because it had only one very weak local competitor for an essential product.

This situation had arisen largely because the company was an acquired subsidiary of a much larger company that had used it as a staging place for executives on their way up. Thus short stays had become almost institutionalised. Most of the staff were thoroughly demoralised and cynical about the role of leadership and virtually ignored it anyway. Undaunted by the brick walls he ran into at every turn early on, Jim made a commitment to staff to stay for at least four years to get the organisation back on the rails again. Then he proceeded to spend time personally in every section of the plant until he knew both the people and the processes well.

He targeted two key sections for initial reform, distribution and sales. But the most important thing he did was to encourage the most enthusiastic operators to come up with new ideas. To give them their head under his direct guidance and to stay with each process, removing the barriers to change as they became evident.

He found, for example, that the distribution system was difficult to change because it was locked into a system of ordering, controlled by one person who had designed it 20 years before and who refused to change any part of it. Although a quite expensive computerised system had been installed, it sat in the corners of offices being used solely by some younger enthusiasts for their own entertainment and personal training. The distribution manager was ultimately sent off to a management training course that included a large component of technology, and by the time he returned, eight weeks later, the new computerised distribution system was up and running, providing the basis on which sales could be reviewed and monitored.

But there were other problems: sales outlets were old fashioned and vertically integrated; not surprisingly, stock was often not available; customer satisfaction was low, and sales staff were less than enthusiastic. Jim allowed the network time to spread word among employees about reforms in the distribution system and actively talked about it in other sections of the plant, as well as his new company newsletter.

In any case the results began to speak for themselves: stock ordering was more reliable; requests for supplies were quickly responded to; staff conferences had been held where each section talked and discussed problems and new ideas. Ultimately, sales outlets were reorganised. Most sales outlets were closed down and relocated in large department stores and the product was made more widely available through other retail outlets. Jim used his old network in sales and marketing to introduce help from the outside, adapting and retraining staff, and refurbishing, reorganising, redistributing and penetrating each nook and cranny of the marketplace to increase production and sales in two years by over 150 per cent. Jim's network was developed through a hands-on involvement with staff in the company. It was the only way to penetrate the barriers that had been built up over years of disappointment and let-down.

Now five years down the track, Jim has fulfilled his promise to staff and has built up a competent management team. He is now looking for another challenge. The parent company wants him to stay, after all, why change a winning formula. The error they made before was to reward failure with promotion, now they want to reward success with stagnation. Jim's network outside the company is extensive. He is a people person with a large network of enthusiastic admirers who know what he has achieved elsewhere and in this present company. He has made sure that word of his success has spread among his peers and, of course, the financial results speak for themselves. He is currently considering a number of very lucrative offers and the parent company will probably lose him because they simply don't understand the basic principles of how to nurture their most important asset, their most innovative and enthusiastic people.

Steeling the future

Many chief executives in today's world need to come out of their ivory towers. Even when they have been with an organisation a long time, they need to understand what is changing both inside and outside the organisation.

Larry, the plant manager of a steel company with thousands of employees, was locked into a very narrow view of the world. Like numerous other executives in the world he inhabited, he had a degree from Newcastle University, which has one of the only courses for mining and metallurgy in the country. Graduates form a close knit group; are almost exclusively male; go into one or two major companies; rise and promote each other through the ranks and give the monolithic steel companies their sameness, their bureaucratic stamp and their conservative, locked-in quality. Faced with falling productivity, a more competitive world and domestic markets and threats of takeovers from the outside, the steel companies are now at a crossroads. They must open their doors and their traditional ways of operating or go to the wall.

As part of this opening up Larry was sent to Japan to inspect Japanese management and was stunned by what he saw. He attended courses in America on new management techniques and many of his preconceptions were shattered as a result. He began to develop a whole new set of contacts – people from disciplines so far distant from mining and metallurgy that at first it was hard to understand their language.

What was a corporate culture, what were human resources, what was networking, information gatekeeping, targeted publics and communication strategies' quality circles? The bottom line for Larry was that within these new "softer" human communications disciplines, from which he had been locked out, lay the key to his own and his organisation's future success. By the time we met him he was ready to allow us to facilitate the massive organisational change process required to turn the company around.

We came to him through his new-found network, which was largely outside the organisation and his own fraternity. The challenge lies ahead but all his senior- and many middle-management staff are also experiencing training of the kind to which Larry was exposed. It is an exciting time as the "soft" and "hard" disciplines prepare to go into business together. Mercifully many of his younger engineering colleagues are going through the same rebirthing process and will eventually reinforce new organisational ideas.

The principle is: chief executives need information. They must be certain they are getting it from the source that is most useful to them. This often means going beyond a supportive close-knit little pond. That source may not increase their comfort level and it will often challenge it. Because of the life they lead, or the people they mix with, the tendency is for them not to know what is really changing in the outside world.

Chief executives must be open, but more than that they must seek out the people who will tell them what is going on, not the people who will tell them what they think they want to hear. These key contacts will often be good networkers themselves across various ponds or else well connected in particular ponds. They will come from both inside and outside the organisation and both should be constantly cultivated, not on the basis of the familiar, but on the basis of what is changing and likely to affect the organisation in the short, medium and long term.

This requires effort, judgement and openness as well as a willingness to diagnose and read the situation closely, so as to see the young man wearing jeans and a T-shirt for what he might be – the brilliant innovator with a mind ready to invent the next widgit; or the woman executive who might pull off deal after deal through patient negotiation rather than a macho knock-'em-down drag-'em-out approach.

Again reciprocity is important. The chief executive has to listen, really listen, as well as talk. He or she must invite interchange and never "punish" the frank and open statement. Nothing will be learned if they invite dialogue and then do nothing or, worse still, punish or betray that exchange. A new style of management for a new kind of challenge is called for, where information is at a premium and networks that carry it are important to understand and be a part of.

C. Looking for Your First Job

In the tight job market that operates today, clearly there will be winners but also losers. It is a regrettable phenomenon that young job-seekers are the most vulnerable group in our society. We know that a majority of jobs given to young people come through personal contact – word of mouth, family or friends. So if you are one of these people seeking a job you know what you have to do. Network – but recognise the strengths or limitations of your own group and work out ways in which you can use what you have got, your launching pad, or how to extend your network beyond your own tight-knit little group.

Growing in the west

Darryl falls into the category of the most vulnerable group. He lives in the western suburbs of Sydney, a long way from many job opportunities, among many others like himself. His mother is a single parent and he has one elder brother and one sister both of whom are working but don't live at home. Darryl's friends are all in the same boat. Their parents are on low incomes and his friends are fairly pessimistic about their chances of getting a job.

But when Darryl left school, he was determined to get a job in spite of the pessimism of the group to which he belonged. So he set about looking before he had completed school. At first he just answered the advertisements, went to the CES office and suffered the same fate as job seekers everywhere who go in cold. He was becoming discouraged when he finally sat down one day and made a list of all the people he knew who might help him. Some of them seemed pretty distant hopes but he still put them down anyway. This is what Darryl's map of contacts looked like, see Figure 11.1.

The group at the top are family. Both Martin and Sally work and were a good source of contacts with their own employers. An uncle in the country was connected but a bit remote. Besides, shearing is a skilled trade and Darryl had no rural background.

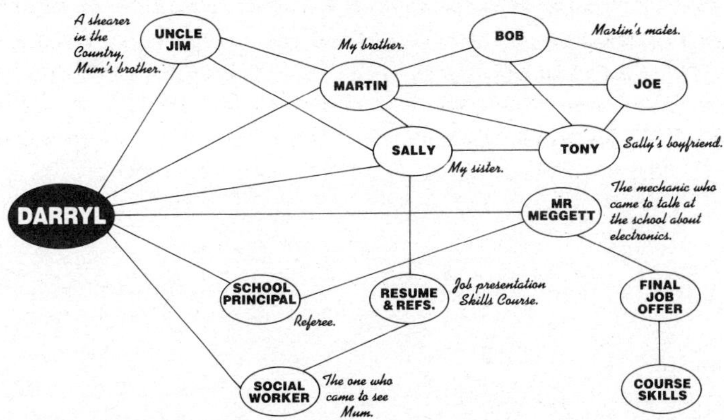

Figure 11.1
Map of Darryl's contacts in looking for a job

Darryl went to see a social worker who helped him put a résumé and references together and referred him to a group who offered training in how to present himself better – what to wear and what to say to a prospective employer. He also visited his brother and sister and left them copies of his résumé and references. He wrote to his uncle in the country. He contacted the school principal, one of his referees, and left a resume with him too.

Then he remembered Mr Meggett, one of the men from a small Parramatta company, who had spoken at the school. He got his address from the school principal and went to see him looking as presentable as possible. Mr Meggett didn't have any jobs vacant, of course, but undaunted, Darryl said he'd work for nothing for a while for the experience and Meggett reluctantly allowed him to stay. He was there a week when one of the apprentices took ill. Darryl filled in, coming in early and staying late to help with the overload. Now he was drawing wages.

A little while later Meggett received a call from a friend who had decided to employ someone but didn't want a "no-hoper". Darryl got that job and was there for two years before going on to train and study in electronics, first at the tech and then at the institute of technology. Mr Meggett's network and his old employer offer him ample part-time work to support him while he is studying.

Curiously enough, not long after his first job offer his sister Sally came up with a similar opportunity. The remarkable thing about directed and purposeful networking is the degree to which opportunities serve to increase and multiply as you become more proficient at making connections. The more connections you make, the more possibilities open up to you. Darryl did not have many leads but he used almost all of the ones he did have. He has learnt that lesson well for the future.

A Matter of Choice

Young graduates looking for their first job are in a much better position to find a job than Darryl. Commerce and economics graduates especially are quickly snapped up and offered jobs in banks and accounting firms. Companies like IBM have had a policy of recruiting graduates with a variety of degrees. Their own company training augments the basic training and performance acquired at university. But many young graduates know little about employment opportunities in their area and less about how to approach the choice of an employer. In the present job market, skills are at a premium so the young graduate can afford to go about choosing his or her first employer fairly systematically.

A recent publication in America, *The Hundred Best Companies to Work for in America*, may point the way towards a new trend where employees assess their employers on the basis of what their expectations are. If this occurs in Australia it will indeed be a dramatic turnaround – and the signs are certainly there. This, of course, will present organisations with an enormous challenge. They will need to meet these new expectations if they are to attract the brightest and best graduates. But our immediate advice is directed to young graduates who can use the networking process to discover the kind of organisation they want to work for that will meet their own career objectives.

When Alexander graduated with a degree in commerce law he figured his first job should be with a medium-sized public or private sector organisation. He also figured that since the world is made up and run by large organisations, working in one would be the only way to find out how they function. If he wanted to go into business on his own some day then basic business and organisational skills would also be learned there. Alexander knew that this is the way to minimise mistakes in making decisions under the guidance of other, more experienced people and at their expense not his own. He also knew that large organisations can afford to carry that risk and they minimise it by building in supervision of young graduates. More importantly from the networking perspective, large organisations provide invaluable contacts and information that are just not available anywhere else.

Alex, in choosing an employer, first decided what kind of a person he was and what kind of environment he would like to work in. Since he would be starting at the bottom of the ladder he also decided how he wanted to be treated, what kind of work he would like to be doing and the kind of people he would like to be associated with. He figured his early experiences could influence a great deal of his future career.

With a good degree he knew he was reasonably in demand, and he approached the recruiting agencies who came to the campus and asked them many specific questions. He was surprised at how frank they were prepared to be. They hadn't encountered many young graduates who asked these kinds of questions before. Mostly people's questions stopped at salary and conditions and didn't go much further than that.

But Alex had had the foresight to ask around among friends and family about their work and what they thought about it during his last two years at university. As a young potential recruit, he found he was no threat to anyone and he was in a good position to hear the truth and ask ingenuous questions. Many of the people he spoke to from within companies were also prepared to give him contacts in other parts of the company and in competitive and non-competitive companies as well.

Like Alex, if you are doing your own research and haven't been referred by the company's recruiters, don't ask for a job – you are now doing "research" and research of this kind is no threat; asking for a job is. Alex never left his first contact without a referral to his second, his second contact without a referral to his third and so on.

On one occasion he heard back through the network that the head of the corporate law department remarked to a colleague over lunch: "Had a good young potential recruit in today. Referred to us by Jones in marketing. He asked a lot of penetrating questions. Jim, do you still have that vacancy in your section?" Although many first jobs are filled through selective recruitment, especially of the best and brightest of graduates, many more jobs are filled through personal contacts – networking.

Having done his research Alex was now in a position to reflect on corporate culture: how it works; what organisations value; what systems they use; who holds power. Many of the more detailed and subtle elements of cultural dynamics will not be available to an outsider, of course. Alex knew he must wait until he became part of the team to understand it slowly, learn to work within it and to make it work for him. And part of the adventure, he knew, would be that voyage of discovery.

There are a few constructs, however, that will greatly help you, as they did Alex, to understand your environment, and each of these is an essential guide-post on your cultural map.

The choice of a company or other organisation will be determined by chemistry, just as the choice of a lover is. How do you judge the organisation you will be compatible with? Look first at the physical environment – what a company wants to say about itself is reflected in its environment. Look at the buildings owned by IBM, Digital, Citicorp and ask yourself what each one says to the world through its buildings, receptionists, its furniture and its accommodation, and its publications. If it values marketing and sales more than personnel and research, you will know by looking at the accommodation given to each of these areas or the budgets allocated to each. Status might be judged by the plushness or otherwise of their respective accommodation. If the overall accommodation is neat and simple, the corporation might want to present a lean and strong image to the world. A plusher environment might indicate that they are doing well and want the world to know. Sometimes image and substance are different and asking some questions, such as how long the company has been established, or looking behind the glossy facade, might be important. Behind the facade of Coles' head office in Melbourne is a very spartan environment reflecting an emphasis on low overheads and profit margins in the retail industry.

Having once got a job you now have the important task ahead: reading the culture from the inside, although reading, of course, is no substitute for experience. Be aware that each organisation has a history and that history has determined what happens today. Ask questions, listen to the storyteller, look and listen and feel your way with sensitivity and learn from experience when you make mistakes. Read *Corporate Cultures* by Kennedy and Deal which will give you some insights into how organisational culture works.

Alex took up a job with a medium-size, newish computer software company – a subsidiary of a larger company certainly, but one that had few bureaucratic layers and that offered a new recruit a range of experiences and opportunities. His boss was a woman who gave him a lot of encouragement and gradually extended his responsibility as his performance gained in quality and breadth. He also felt he could go to her for advice, and regular case conferences and project discussions gave him accelerated opportunities to learn and made him feel he was never isolated in making decisions.

But what of the graduate who is not as lucky or whose homework was not as thorough as Alex's?

Making Mistakes

If you make a mistake, don't despair. Life is full of unexpected and exciting opportunities. The main thing is to open yourself to them and to work to increase the chances that they will happen for you. If you are a serious networker and, therefore, serious about success, your life will be built on a series of interlocking contacts and experiences that can circulate and be recirculated constantly throughout your life.

A final word of warning if you plan to leave an organisation because you are unhappy there. Never leave under a cloud, if you can possibly avoid it. If you do leave under a cloud, don't worry unduly. False starts are not at all unusual. For some people, getting the sack has meant the beginning of great new opportunities. But don't circulate that information yourself. Often people are their own worst enemy in this regard. In their anxiety to prove they were "right", they talk a lot about how awful the company was and what a hard time their boss gave them. In doing so they run the risk of telling a possible future employer that they are disloyal or might have certain inadequacies.

So move on gracefully and choose the best time to quit the scene if you're not happy with it. But make sure you are giving it enough time to be sure it can't work. Don't wait until you get so frustrated they ask you to leave after a blow up or row. The good networker is cool and thoughtfully strategic about such matters.

Young graduates have very little access to power and information but can begin by assessing what they want and looking for an organisational setting that will meet their needs. They may not have much to go on except their own judgement, their own powers of observation and their openness to others. Yet these should all be used strategically for maximum advantage.

Checklist

Chapter 11

- Networking is an ideal way to loosen up organisations so they can be more adaptive and faster moving.
- Much of the real business in organisations goes on in the organisation's complex web of interlocking relationships.
- Taking stock of these networks is as important to the success of the organisation as taking stock of personal networks is to the success of the individual.
- These interlocking relationships, the image and history of an organisation are all key factors in understanding its culture and how it currently works and its potential to work differently.
- You can build your own personal networks in such a way that they help you to climb the corporate ladder.
- In looking for a job, the more connections you make the greater the number of possibilities that will open up to you. You should not be afraid to step across into new ponds.
- Sometimes a networking research process can uncover the information you need about job alternatives and other's experiences.
- When leaving an organisation, try not to leave under a cloud but do not be unduly worried if you do. False starts are not unusual and often open up new opportunities.
- It is a changing world; some of your old contacts can be extremely valuable in the future. Don't neglect them.

Chapter 12
Some Further Pointers to Success
Using Networking if you are...

D. A Community Worker

Throughout this book we have pointed to the difference between issue or community networks and given emphasis to the concept of personal networks. We have also discussed certain similarities between the two. The following example brings the two together and demonstrates the way each may be worked in with the other.

The smallest pond of all for many people is the one that traps them geographically according to their place of residence. Millions of people get trapped by their location, particularly women in the early days of marriage and childbearing. Marilyn's experience is the story of someone who managed to enhance the life of those in the community amongst whom she lived, and at the same time to extend her own personal success through, with and well beyond it. She is still widening her contacts as her personal success grows.

Chereyville estate is part of a vast spread of suburbs that stretches like the tentacles of an octopus across the suburban plain of Melbourne's western suburbs. Marilyn was one of a number of new Chereyville residents, where there were no shops when she took up residence, no school, no public transportation. Everyone had young children or was newly married and starting families and most were on low incomes.

Like the other women on the estate, Marilyn was grateful to have a home of her own. But the isolation and the sense of strangeness among people she did not know was an unexpected blow. The depressing effect of that alienation hung like a pall over all those neat lawns, tiled roofs and small gardens, gardens that struggled in the relentless sun to grow on a plain that had been so recently devastated by the developer's bulldozers. Marilyn talked to her neighbours about how they could improve the situation. They in turn spoke to their neighbours and a small meeting was held at Marilyn's house to discuss an action plan. A group was eventually formed, with Marilyn as its leader.

The first thing the group decided to do was to call the director of the Housing Ministry and some other government officials, to ask them to a meeting. The objective was to discuss who was responsible for the provision of public facilities and where they could get help to provide other private facilities. A network for community action had been formed. Instead of a small meeting, the group expanded so that a large church hall in the nearest centre had to be hired. The Director of Housing attended the first meeting.

Following the meeting Marilyn was appointed, on a small part-time salary, to act as a community worker on the estate. Soon after that she started a childcare centre using one of the houses on the estate that the Housing Ministry allocated for that purpose. An extension was also built onto the house to provide a large meeting room for other groups, adult education, drama, music, scouts and guides, a sports club and just a place for information exchange. Picnics and other activities were also organised from this centre and the men formed an Apex and a Lions Club and began to hold meetings there.

The activities that Marilyn organised were numerous and wide ranging, and after several years the Housing Ministry offered her a more formidable challenge - the opportunity to work with the problems of inner-city high-rise public housing.

The newspapers used the group of tower block apartments, to which Marilyn was assigned, as a constant source of sensational copy, recounting stories of how women had been raped in the corridors and babies flung from balconies by distraught mothers. The cost of repairing the constant damage from vandalism on the estate was also prohibitive. Only the most desperate low income tenants, who had no other choice, lived there. It was clear something had to done.

The first thing that Marilyn did was to make over one of the ground-floor apartments into a meeting place or clearing house for each apartment block. A general survey of complaints was carried out. The residents were then organised into small groups based on common concerns (networked), floor by floor. Surprisingly, most people didn't know each other. A meeting with residents from each building was eventually held, but only when enough people felt sufficiently comfortable with one another to meet in a larger group.

The Housing Ministry's plans for refurbishing the apartments were kept on display and residents were encouraged to visit and comment on the plans as they proceeded, and to discuss them with each other. They did, indeed, make many positive suggestions for change that really worked. The outcomes of this networking process were quietly miraculous and they led to important changes in how the blocks were administered and refurbished. Importantly for Marilyn, however, her capacity and courage to take on such a tough assignment - to jump from her local suburb to a job in a bigger pond - led to her present success.

Ten years after speaking at her first meeting in Chereyville, Marilyn's children are now 16, 15 and 12. She has been promoted to a senior position in the Housing Ministry as the director of community liaison, where she is busy passing on her networking skills to others. She has trained most of the ministry's housing officers in new ways of relating to their tenants and estate management, which encourages residents to run their own affairs and take responsibility for their own lives. The cost, incidentally, for vandalism is at its lowest ever on all estates. The direct cost savings is counted in millions of dollars.

Marilyn is still a relatively young woman whose success speaks for itself. She is a good communicator. She constantly looks for new opportunities and new contacts and is likely to move in to a wider variety of ponds.

E. A Small Businessperson

Tom and Maryanne worked together in one of Australia's largest advertising agencies. Over a period of two years they developed many new advertising ideas, most of which were rejected by the company's senior executives because they were too radical. Maryanne, particularly, felt the advertising fostered by the company was out of date and sexist and it was time for a change, if only to acknowledge the market realities of the growing buying power of women and their changing roles.

The day eventually came, of course, when creativity had to have its head and both Tom and Maryanne left the company. A client followed them to their new small office, which was all they could afford, and the team developed a stunningly different campaign for half the previous cost. Tom and Maryanne's new company's name was ATOM and news of its success spread through its developing network of contacts in the industry. ATOM also attracted other creative, zany artists and people with ideas, as well as dissatisfied clients from other agencies.

A success story? Well, no, not exactly. Although, through both talent and contacts, the company grew and appeared to prosper, because neither Tom nor Maryanne had good business or financial skills, they ran into trouble. This meant that they eventually came close to losing everything because they neglected this side of their business. Eventually Maryanne's network came good with a competent financial advisor who put the company on a more secure footing. Just in time they instituted financial systems to keep track of cash flows and budgeting and installed a financial controller to manage the company's business affairs.

The fact is that small businesspeople are enormously vulnerable in the marketplace. Although there are many of them, many also go out of business and this loss represents an enormous waste of talent and opportunity.

One of the major problems associated with small business is the kind of people who become attracted to it. Gumpert and Boyd's research on this subject, published in the November/December 1984 *Harvard Business Review*, reveals that small businesspeople tend, by nature, to be rugged individualists. They often leave large corporations because they can't stand the delays and the bureaucratisation. They want to do things their way. This means that they tend to be loners. This tendency makes them vulnerable, lacking in the support that networks generally can provide but particularly the close-knit web of contacts that many people weave in the working environment. Because we know also that loneliness and stress are closely associated, and prolonged stress leads to illness, they are vulnerable on that score as well.

So what do small businesspeople need to do to protect themselves against these dangers? First they need all the encouragement they can get from their family and friends and they should set things up so that this is likely to happen. The last thing a small businessperson needs is for their marriage to break down because their husband/wife couldn't stand the strain and the worry of mortgaging the house to finance the business! We suggest, too, that friends or acquaintances who might, for whatever reason, undermine your confidence, need to be assessed in a new light. Who needs a Jeremiah when you are struggling to maintain your own energy level and enthusiasm?

Small businesspeople should also think carefully about the diversity of people who can help them in their business and seek the right advice. The advice we give elsewhere about talking only to the people who make one feel comfortable applies especially here. New markets and opportunities might be close at hand, but if they are not part of a person's network then they might as well not be there at all.

We know that small businesses grow into bigger businesses. So small businessmen and women need to extend their contacts to reach new markets, employ new people, build teams, develop commitment and keep their information right up to the minute. We also know that this has to be done through an increasing, expanding and complex linkage of communications, all of which will be centred on helping the company prosper. This means that the natural loner will need to learn how to become a leader of a diverse team. Working informally in the network for the good of the new company, or coming together to form a larger group. Whatever the style of operation, remember, "No one can do anything important alone".

A good example of a man who has grown a company from a small business to a larger business, at the same time maintaining the advantages of "small is beautiful", is Peter Fritz. Peter Fritz was one of the recipients of the BHP Awards for the Pursuit of Excellence, and the managing director of Technical Computing and Graphics. Peter's style is entrepreneurial and he works constantly on a network approach, building up contacts throughout government, industry, academia and with other small businesses and in export markets. He has used this network and his undoubted business success to build an excellent reputation in the industry.

He has combined entrepreneurship in hi-tech, leading edge technology (a high-risk industry by its very nature) with an adequate web of networked support both for the company as a whole and for each of his individual ventures. In 10 years his company (which is made up of a number of small self-contained honeycombed cells, rather like one of our networked diagrams, supported at the centre) has impressed the Japanese so much that he is the only non-Japanese company to whom Seiko have ever given an overseas distributionship.

The Fritz style of hi-tech venture investment is based on profit-sharing for those involved in the invention and in bringing the work to fruition, but in a managed and supported environment. Peter believes in service to customers, open communication and sorting out problems as they arise. His style of small-business development may well be more suited to the Australian risk-shy culture than many of the more flamboyant high-risk ventures that can be found in the United States hi-tech venture industry.

F. An Entrepreneur

Above all, the entrepreneur is a finder of opportunity and a maker of deals who stretches across the visible and the invisible boundaries that contain "normal" behaviour. The entrepreneur is a pond-jumper and often an extremely good "crossroads" networker.

The "magic" of the hi-tech industry comes from the breathless enthusiasm of an entrepreneur whose expectation is that much larger than normal profits can be made out of innovations and developing inventions into multimillion-dollar enterprises. There are a number of very important lessons for entrepreneurs in general and hi-tech networking in particular – not the least of which is that in this industry, although there are big profits to be made, they are not necessarily quick profits. If you go into this business you are in it for the long haul and the trust people have in you, and the contacts you develop over time can make the difference between success or failure.

As Peter Fritz has found, many of the secrets of new technology are locked away in laboratories, universities, research institutes or in small companies without enough capital to develop their products. Finding such opportunities requires a different style of operation than that required of the normal small-business entrepreneur, or entrepreneurial activity carried out within large organisations. Large organisations have recently begun to recognise this however, as is evidenced by the terms "skunkworks" (see Peters and Waterman, *In Search of Excellence)* and "intrapreneuring" (see the book with this title by Pinchot – and also the excellent discussion on internal entrepreneurship in *Change Masters* by Rosabeth Moss

Kanter). Fundamentally the same sort of processes are involved: the finding of opportunities locked away in untapped minds and remote corners of the organisation, and the crossing of formal and informal boundaries inside the organisation – going beyond the usual role expectations – that tend to constrain "normal" people. How else can one do these things other than through networking? Wherever he or she is, the successful entrepreneur succeeds through extending his or her network and sources of information, well beyond the original group and the traditional norms of the situation.

Over the years those like Peter Fritz, and others serving their apprenticeship in this entrepreneurial activity, have had to learn sophisticated networking skills. Although many of the business managers serve time (after gaining their law, science or economics/accounting degrees) in large organisations that equip them for financial and legal analysis, the other essential processes of becoming an entrepreneur, especially in hi-tech areas, have to be learned on the job.

These processes include: a capacity to judge people and their skills, reliability and management expertise; the capacity to find the right venture, which might be hiding in an academic research institute or sithin the heads of entrepreneurs within a large organisation or a suburban garage; the capacity to put the right combination of skills together, in the form of a group of people, who can make it all happen.

The literature on innovation is full of historical examples of inventions and other opportunities, which found a champion who knew how to put the deal together, so that a multi-million-dollar business could grow out of it. The invention is only part of the story. The deal must be right in terms of compatibility and agreements between people, and the invention has to been found in the first place. The advice now so often given to people investing in this area is to invest in people not in the technology, because the right team can make a success of almost anything!

The combination of skills required for success in innovative new ventures rarely lies in one person. So teams of people assemble and reassemble constantly for this purpose and develop both closed and open networks. Open at some periods when they are looking for new ventures or people; closed when they are finalising a deal or working on highly confidential scientific processes, when only the most trusted advice and associates are allowed information. Interesting, within any large organisation, are processes that are going on over time. There is a constant alignment and realignment and shifts in power between the potential players – colleagues wanting to be seen with the product or ideas champion; top management wanting to "godfather" the cause (see Peters and Waterman, *In Search of Excellence*); or those who definitely do not want to be associated.

The work is hard and the hours are long, but the risks can be great and potential rewards enormous, especially for the independent entrepreneur. People learn the hard way, get bitten, come back and start again. Fortunes are made and lost and still they go on looking for opportunities – like mining for gold, but not in the earth. Out there among people and institutions, talking, making contacts, socialising, working in conferences, workshops, always on the lookout for this year's multimillion-dollar opportunity. This year's Apple computer or software package, next year's bio-tech wonder drug or medical technology.

It is within the hi-tech entrepreneurial industry that the words "intellectual property" have developed their greatest meaning. This is, of course, a subset of the information economy – with clear dollar signs at the end of the rainbow. In Australia the hi-tech venture industry is relatively new and its success will ultimately depend on how well it learns to break into overseas markets. This will require cross-cultural activity, the Netmapping of relationships, and the building of overseas networks, marketing and distribution systems that will work effectively to support the parent group in Australia.

For a country that has suffered the insecurity engendered by its "tyranny of distance", this will require extensive changes in the way in which it views the world and operates within it. Overcoming a fear of people and places that are different; reading cultures; developing trusted new contacts; checking and rechecking strange networks; finding links, however, tenuous; working cooperatively with colleagues to share experiences and contacts and much more besides, are all skills that will need to be acquired by the serious networker.

It is for this reason that the next chapter deals more extensively with the cross cultural issue.

Checklist

Chapter 12

- Community networking skills require access to many different ponds and the results can be dramatic – welding together people with disparate backgrounds to achieve a common purpose.
- Small businesspeople tend to be loners and are, therefore, vulnerable to stress.
- But nobody can do anything important alone and it is, therefore, crucial that they look carefully at the networks in which they are embedded and the opportunities that are opened up.
- Small businesspeople need a supportive network of family and friends.
- They need contacts in a number of different ponds. As the business grows, they need to build a team of people with different expertise.
- Networking is crucial, both to the independent entrepreneur and the "intrapreneur" inside an organisation.
- To tap into the secrets and the potentials of innovative people and to be in touch in the right places at the right time, all requires so much more than just dwelling in a small semi-stagnant pond.
- In addition, entrepreneurial networking is crucial to pull together the teams of talent necessary to make things work and to find the right people and circumstances to put together the deals to bring in the rewards.

Chapter 13

Going Places – Home and Abroad

Networking Success in the Global Ecomony

Australia, America, Great Britain, Canada, New Zealand, Fiji and South Africa are all societies in a state of rapid cultural change. This is because they are what Professor Eric Wilmot calls a "polygeneric society" – a society made up of a number of cultural groups whose primary culture originated somewhere else.

Each racial group in these societies is in the process of "embeddling" one another, to use one of Wilmot's terms. Embeddling is that process of influencing and changing each other on a day to day basis until we eventually become a new cultural group. Wilmot describes this process by reference to an analogy of the famous Russian dolls, each of which fits neatly into the next one, and so on many times over. Each doll is a whole unto itself but each is a part of the whole. Australia, he believes, is "The Last Experiment" in the embeddling process. (The 1986 Boyer Lectures, ABC.)

The fact is that in Australia nearly half the population have arrived here since World War II. About a third of us had parents whose first language was other than English.

Helen, for example, is a woman of Greek origin whose mother speaks only Greek and whose father learned the English language and spoke for both of them. Helen married an Australian of Anglo-Saxon origin and her children's awareness of their Greek origins, although strong, is less strong than their identification with Australia and its culture.

Helen's father Dimitrius (Danny to his Australian friends), has built up a successful shoe manufacturing business and has done it, first, with the help of his Greek friends but secondly with the help of many older Australians. How has he achieved this? He cultivated his bank manager, a fourth generation Aussie, asking him to dinner at his home. He joined the local Chamber of Commerce and met many businessmen and women there. He made friends with suppliers, with accountants and lawyers, and he employs a number of different cultural groups in his business.

His son-in-law, for his part, has taken a special interest in Helen's Greek heritage. He has been adopted by other members of the Greek community, he has visited Greece and has gained richly from that cultural encounter.

These individuals have certainly been busy "embeddling" each other's cultures and each has a great deal to gain from doing so. But for every story like this one there are many full of conflict and anguish. The important thing for the networker is to understand that we live among people who have cultural differences, and that these differences are important to them. More importantly from a personal success perspective, each other's culture offers a range of new opportunities. There are new and different ponds. To ignore them is to miss out on what they have to offer.

Various ethnic groups are entering the professions, and business, and becoming rich, famous and powerful. When they get together they can form large, but at the same time, reasonably close-knit networks that tend to cut across a range of old institutions and their associations can be very powerful indeed. More complex still, within such groups one faction sometimes doesn't see eye to eye with another. The Greek Orthodox community in Australia, for example, is divided between two groups, traditionalists and progressives. Understanding these kinds of complexities will make the difference between success and failure in gaining access to these networks.

WHAT DO YOU MEAN, 'IT'S TIME WE CAME DOWN OUTA THE TREES'?
We've got a very civilised network running here...
I'll take my chances
KNIGHT

So if you want to marry into, do business with, live alongside, get information, service, advice from, or communicate with people in the Irish, Lebanese, Italian, Aboriginal or other communities, there are sensitivities involved that will need to be recognised and carefully observed, particularly if this Australian polygeneric society is to become a "united nation".

Until recently, the notion of culture was a secret – a secret in that most of us don't think about the hidden cultural forces that influence and determine our lives. So for some people it didn't exist. Such forces were often regarded instead as part of "human nature". Yet one cultural group's "human nature" is another's *bête noir*.

A Matter of Perception

Some people have understood the difference between human nature and culture long before it made its way into more popular understanding.

Robert Thomas, the former chief executive of the Australian Industry Development Corporation, walked the length of the long main street of Rabaul seeking information on how the native people of Papua New Guinea insured their vehicles.

The year was 1959 and his walk was part of a much larger mission, namely, to investigate, on behalf of the Reserve Bank of Australia, the need for and the use of credit by the indigenous people of Papua New Guinea This particular mission had enormous long term significance for the Papua New Guinea Economy.

Bob was accompanied in this mission by a young anthropologist. Although it was early days in terms of a more general understanding of the importance of cultural differences, this tough assignment, if it was to succeed, needed a different perspective to any that had gone before.

Bob and his assistant for instance, found that there were 80 trucks under individual "native" ownership and that, although insurance was compulsory, not one of the insurance companies was prepared to insure the vehicles. "The natives' don't look after property" they maintained.

Eventually Bob's quest led him to the office of the agent for the South British Insurance Company, who, it transpired, had cornered all the business for insuring the "native-owned" vehicles in Rabaul. The Agent summed up how he had cornered the market like this: "the 'natives' look after the vehicles they own better than Europeans. It's a myth, that they don't want to own assets and that they don't take care of them when they do. I don't mind the other companies believing this, since it means I get all the business."

A Matter of Credit

By establishing wide contacts among the indigenous people, Bob and his assistant also uncovered the prevailing European myths about their use of money. Contrary to popularly held European beliefs, for example, the indigenous people did have savings but they kept them stored away in their own houses, since they had never developed trust in the banks.

The Europeans, for their part, believed that it was useless to use banks or to establish facilities to provide credit for the indigenous people, because they would not pay back the loans. There was, of course, some truth to this. The indigenous people saw the large European owned banks as remote, wealthy institutions that could afford to take losses arising from default.

However when, as a result of Bob's report to the Reserve Bank, savings and loan institutions were organised as cooperative village banks, the outcomes were very different. Because the village people had the responsibility for running these institutions, they recognised that loans could only be made from deposits made by other 'natives' of the village. Within the indigenous culture debts were required to be repayed. Not to do so would have brought swift and serious reprisals.

A Matter of Judgement

There are two points to this story. The first is that cross-cultural understanding and networking within that context are not new and that people who wanted real results made the effort long before the 70's and 80's. The second is that success in the cross-cultural stakes means clearing our minds of our own cultural judgements and values in order to see things through the eyes of the group we wish to understand.

Bob, for example, looked for the culturally specific indicators that would give him the right clues to how the indigenious people used money. He also networked his way among the key people who could give him that clearer picture of the real situation, not those who would reinforce his or their own prejudices and preconceptions.

The lesson? Penetrating a culture always has and still does require sensitivity of a high order, the right information and the right contacts – but these have to be approached with an open mind and a sensitive appreciation of cultural differences. The principles of networking remain the same. The point is, however, that different cultures and different values operating within those cultures determine the approach we take towards personal networking if we really want to succeed.

As the two examples above illustrate, the key to your personal success might hang on understanding how to 'map' the culture you want to influence or penetrate. Once you understand how to 'map' a culture, you can then move in there with confidence to manage the change process, or get that order, job, contract, project or research grant, marry the person of your choice or otherwise take advantage of an opportunity that might lie within the new pond.

Cultural mapping is simply this: Learning to read the key differences in identity between groups, nations or organisations with accuracy and then learning how to adapt your own behaviour, so that you respect those differences. At the same time you must learn how to take advantage of what you know about those differences. But to do this you will also need to take risks. Networking requires a sense of adventure and a capacity to cope with and enjoy change. Bob and his assistant could have stayed in the club comfortably drinking with Europeans and adopting their perceptions. But they chose to do things differently.

Coming to grips with an identity that might be different from your own or that you may only perceive to be different, is a personal challenge and it requires effort. It may even create a sense of anxiety (risk). But the effort will pay off in the end. Without this sense of adventure to jump into different, bigger ponds, there would be no links made between people who need to know one another or to work together on a project – there would be no innovation, no sharing or publishing of new discoveries, and no entrepreneurship. And as we have said before, in the information society, sharing information and new ideas is the essence of success in the future.

If you don't develop some perspective on the cultural signposts or systems that will help you understand how life is lived in the larger ponds and how to make your way in them, then you might as well stay where you are, because we can tell you now, networking won't work for you.

Organisational Culture

Just as nations have cultures and groups within them, so, too, do organisations. Organisational culture is that quality that makes an organisation distinctive. It is its vision, the things its says about itself, its leadership, the kinds of people who work within it and the kinds of services it provides. ESSO is different to Qantas; a health department very different from a transport department.

Organisations are themselves influenced by the culture of the time – such as social and economic circumstances and the national culture, so they don't exist in a vacuum.

Mapping the organisational culture is an essential prerequisite to organisational change, and we have described more fully in the previous chapter how some people operate through networks to change their organisation's culture and to get things moving or foster their own success.

What Culture Means

The popular and systematic study of culture is relatively new. It has aided a more widespread understanding of how nations, groups and communities operate and what historic, geographic and social factors are likely to influence this behaviour and, indeed, the outcome of events.

In one sense, and for our purposes at least, culture can be described as the way in which a society builds its formal and informal communication links, providing access to information, protection, as well as the distribution of power, goods and services to its members. Once you understand culture in this way, its connection with and importance to networking becomes immediately apparent.

Even the 'embeddling' process operates differently from one culture to another. Some cultures assimilate newcomers quickly and easily. For others the twain never really meets. Take, for example, Fiji, the Fijians and the Indians in Fiji who live separate lives within the one country. Not much embeddling going on there.

So group behaviour operates on a more or less systematic basis and within certain well defined and less well defined even mythical constructs. Culture determines what and who we are and why we do things the way we do them. Culture is a combination of our race, genes, history (the dead speaking to the living), geography, the major significant events which have occurred and the belief systems we hold and the stories we like to tell about ourselves. You do not need to take on the identity of a new group to communicate with it or to communicate within it. But if you wish to understand the people who belong to that new group or to have them understand and respect you, you must "flow" with these differences – open your mind and suspend judgement about differences in behaviour and style.

Networks and Australian Export Earnings

According to Shimper Kumou of the University of Tokyo:

"The final and greatest social impact of the information revolution will be a synthesis of western and eastern thought to form the guiding ideal for a new global social order."

In the global economy each culture is moving closer to one another. As a result we are all becoming more aware of our own cultural identity and considering the implications of closer communications and interdependence for the future. This is not because it will give us a warm, fuzzy feeling. Far from it. Economic survival is at stake and those who don't take the trouble to understand how these interdependencies influence each other have their head in the sand and are increasingly vulnerable to the worst impacts of change.

Andrew has just taken his first trip to Japan. He is one of 16 Australian orchid growers who took a group tour organised by a leading Japanese orchid grower to culminate in attendance at the world orchid-growers' conference.

Consider the following:

The group did not develop a strategy as to how they would market themselves or their products to the Japanese. Except for one or two members of the group, they did not understand how the Japanese do business or what cultural forces and strengths and weaknesses they were up against. They did not meet prior to departure. They tended to see themselves in competition with each other for the Japanese market.

The trip was beautifully organised and their Japanese hosts were extremely friendly, courteous and helpful. Nothing was too much trouble.

But there were many things that happended that Andrew still does not understand and he is aware that the group could have done better if it had understood more clearly what their own strategy should be in relation to the Japanese.

The group, for example, attended auctions where new plant species were being sold. The Japanese, for some reason which Andrew still does not understand, refused to sell to the Australians. The species went to their Japanese colleagues. The message may be that the Australians needed a Japanese broker to do their bidding. It may be that the Japanese did not want the species to go out of the country to their competitors but were prepared to sell to each other. Whatever the case, the Australians did not know. Nor did they know how to do business in that environment – or adequately prepare themselves for that challenge.

Does it sound familiar?

The reason is that Australians still tend to be locked into a pre-information society view of the world. They see themselves in isolation – not as a united network. In the orchid growers case, they do not appreciate that what they are putting at stake is a small national industry capable of developing considerable national wealth and export earnings, and eventual individual survival within that industry.

Criticisms of cross-cultural sensitivity are not all on one side, of course. Japanese corporations have experienced considerable difficulty establishing themselves in the Australian environment. The Japanese banks are probably the most vulnerable since they are competing for business among a tight 'old boy network' which has built up trust among customers over many years. Good Australian personnel in the banking sector are also in strong demand and dissatisfied employees, who see no future prospects within a Japanese organisation, or where cultural differences make life difficult, are unlikely to stay too long.

The Group

It is these very strengths in Japan which work against the Japanese in other environments. The Japanese are pragmatic; they are not individualistic but are oriented towards group harmony. No one person will make a decision without reference to the group and that process takes a long time. But they will not need endless meetings to hammer out group cohesion itself – it is understood that the group process will eventually prevail. This may not mean that the leader of a Japanese group doesn't necessarily know what he or she wants. If he or she does, his/her task will be to wait until the group reads his/her mind – a subtle and long term process. But recall that the links are actually there and in place – the group is a relatively close-knit network. The leader will not move or make the final decision before this group process is complete, and when it is the action and strategy behind the decision will be economically powerful as a result. It will carry the commitment of the group.

Getting our Act Together

But some of us are learning. Unlike the orchid growers, Fred went to Japan having done his homework. Doing business with the Japanese wasn't new to him, he'd had his fingers burnt in the past and he wasn't going to make the same mistake twice. He took an interpreter and he prepared for a long stay. He knew they wanted his product. He knew it was good and he suspected they couldn't get it elsewhere, but he wasn't sure, so there were risks involved.

Day after day of negotiations ensued. Fred arrived at the Japanese firm at 9 o'clock each morning and sat there until business began. Sometimes nothing started until 11am. People came in and out of the meetings, sometimes they left him sitting there alone. Long (hour-long sometimes) silences were part of the experience so were conversations in Japanese dialect unknown to his interpreter.

Days went by. He had dinner with some of them and laughed and joked out of hours. He never got drunk and never compromised himself. Still days went by. He stuck to his original price, terms of sale and got the contract legally signed before he left the country. But it took nearly two weeks of his life to pull off a contract agreement that in the West would have taken half a day.

What it takes is what it takes.

Japanese Business

If recent strong criticism by Professor Gregory Clark, a long time Japanese resident and professor of international business and economics at Tokyo's Sophia university, is any guide, Australians are in deep trouble in the cross cultural stakes.

Speaking in an interview to Business Review Weekly (April 26, 1986), Clark is quoted as saying that it is almost impossible for a foreigner to penetrate the Japanese business scene without a fluency in the language and the culture. Yet Australian companies persist in sending non-Japanese speaking workers to the country for short periods, only to be surprised at their poor results.

He quotes Comalco's recent disastrous investment in Showa Aluminum in which they lost more than $100 million, as an example of a company out of its depth in Japanese corporate culture. According to Clark, even if Australia embarked on a similar program now, it would be ten years behind its competitors.

Not all observers agree with Clark and there are numerous examples of business being done through trade officials and individual Australian companies which are evidence of a more intelligent cross cultural approach. But it might take five or six years to see a significant change overall for Australia. We need long term strategies. Short term solutions will never work when dealing with the Japanese.

For an Australian firm to succeed in exporting to Japan, the network will be one of a few vital components that can only be developed when it understands how this is done in Japan. The Japanese social cohesion and group-centrism implies that the firm in question must, in developing a useful network, cultivate a longer-term "non-one-time-only" relationship with all organisations there that will be helpful to the promotion of the firm's exports. These organisations could be the importer–wholesaler or a network of regional retailing chains. They could be a joint-venture partner. They could be their bankers (Australian, Japanese, even American) and/or Austrade Tokyo office. The important thing is that this firm develops a viable on-going working relationship with any of these key actors in its Japanese export strategy map, for the acquisition of useful market and other information and the promotion and distribution of its exports. This may hence be a time-consuming process that also requires the firm's representatives to be sensitive to cultural differences and for which the intervention of bilingual, cross-culturally sensitive intermediaries (for example Japanese trading firms) might prove critically important. The significance of the language is especially important in Japan, because the language itself explains and embodies much of the Japanese culture and for which there are no exact English equivalent phrases, because there are no equivalent cultural concepts and sets of behaviours. Once you understand the language, you understand the culture.

So it might take Australian companies five or six years to seal the significant links with Japanese business, and this requires long-range strategies, not short ad hoc development. To succeed Australians need yet again to observe the Japanese way of doing things and work in tandem with it. The Japanese have long been practising networking at home and abroad. Their successes in the world market have been attributed, in part, to the extensive networks they have established for the gathering of useful and often critically important market information and the distribution of their exports. These networks may include trading firms, banks, sole distributors, wholesalers, retailers, advertising agents and market research firms, etcetera.

In short, and at the risk of repetition, to network successfully in Japan the exporters, be they Australian or American, need to approach it so they follow Japanese-style group dynamics. For example, if they have absolutely no contact there to begin with, they should get the help of a go between (a trading company, an export marketing consultant, Austrade, Japan Trade Center, an Australian or Japanese bank) and establish a beach head in Japan. They should then cultivate patiently a long-term relationship with contacts there, with a view to forming a "group" relationship with them. From among them the firms' sole distributor or a joint venture partner may eventuate, providing them the benefit of their wide networks.

For the Japanese the power of networking may take on a different, more individualistic character as their society changes rapidly. From a growing number of examples we believe this is an accelerating phenomenon in Japan in spite of the strong dependency on the group. It may be that the Japanese, in time, will adapt the best of both systems and accommodate the differences faster than we will. They have, after all, become famous for their incredible adaptability to change. Armies of English teachers are presently being imported into Japan to teach the English language to Japanese adults, so there is clearly a recognition of the need to teach more people English than there has been in the past.

But to what extent is Kumou's vision of a new global social order realistic when the East and the West, the North and South, work on entirely different constructs, universes and mindsets? To communicate properly, not just superficially, from one universe of reality to another, all actions and interpretations of those actions must be referred, as De Bono in *Conflicts* puts it, "to the universe in which it is taking place". In other words, you cannot judge one set of actions in one universe or culture by the values or reference points in your own.

The Japanese know this better than anyone. They have learned to network effectively into many cultures. We need to learn to make our own cultural adjustments so we link effectively into theirs. Cross-cultural communications is now a fact of life. How well or how badly we do it will to a large extent determine our future.

Checklist

Chapter 13

- Australia is a polygeneric society – one where many cultures are constantly influencing one another.
- We also live in a global economy where there are countless opportunities where each culture can learn to work more closely together.
- Other cultural groups within our culture offer a range of new opportunities.
- If you want access to these groups you must understand their particular sensitivities and cultural differences.
- Learning to "map" a culture is the best way to gain that access.
- This means clearing your mind of cultural judgements and values to see things through the eyes of the groups you wish to access.
- Each different culture will require a different application of this principle.
- This PROCESS requires effort and risk taking. It may not be a comfortable process.
- In the information society, it is the only way to gain access to other groups, markets and new information.
- You do not need to take on the identity of a new group to communicate with it or within it.
- The essential differences between Japanese and Australian culture is the Japanese close-knit group orientation compared to our looser individualistic and competitive way of relating.

- Australia still has a long way to go in successfully doing business with the Japanese.

- The best way of dealing with that problem is to:

a. cultivate long-term "group" relationships with key actors in the Japanese export strategy map

b. develop long-term strategies

c. expect that rewards will flow after time and effort

d. understand the importance of language

e. enlist the use of a go-between or cultural broker in the early stages

f. establish a beach head in Japan.

Chapter 14
Networks and World Leadership
"Japan versus the United States"

In this book we have described the process of an individual networking his or her way to success as a timely phenomenon, given impetus by the information revolution and capable of opening all sorts of opportunities for everyone.

Assumptions about values and cultural differences underlying this statement could be open to question. We ourselves have considered these assumptions carefully, because to a large extent our approach could be challenged by a different view of the world that has worked extremely well for the Japanese.

The "absorb and adapt", the strong and tight, inward group cohesion that comes with tightlyknit networks and often "locked-in" situations have all been part of the amazing Japanese success story. Networking, in the way we have described it, has not. The Japanese use networks for information but the flow tends to be one way into the group. They take but they don't give much back. But if one studies the experience of individual Japanese young people, dramatic change is afoot which is likely to alter Japanese values and behaviour. This is also likely to have important long term economic outcomes.

Genichi

After Genichi graduated with an MBA from Harvard, he returned to work in Japan as one of the new group of *sarariman* (young, highly qualified Japanese managers). Eight years later he was still with the company, as one would expect in Japan (since lifetime employment with one company is the norm).

Although Genichi found the Japanese culture very supportive and group oriented, he had also experienced a taste of the more open American environment. His old student contacts in America, with whom he kept in touch over the years, were speeding ahead in the fast-track executive lane. Their performance, he noted, was judged by their capacity to generate profits – the bottom line. But Genichi found himself engaged more in internal salesmanship and negotiation than in external business activities. Although Genichi had been one of the best in his class at Harvard, he could see no guaranteed opportunities for advancement in his company.

Eventually he and his wife and children booked their passage back to the States and discussed the problem with some of his former classmates. This visit spawned an opportunity – an offer to set up a subsidiary new hi-tech company in Japan, with a large personal shareholding as part of the deal.

The risks were considerable, of course. If Genichi failed he could not go back to his old company unless he was prepared to accept a substantial demotion and a drop in salary. This action risked his security in old age since only meagre provision is made for old age pensions under Japanese social security arrangements. But Genichi's sense of adventure and confidence in his own ability and imagination finally won out. He now has a thriving business. Americans, Australians and Japanese work for his company in a truly cross cultural environment.

The company has incorporated some of the best aspects of Japanese organisational culture – quality circles, group discussions – with some of the dynamics and speed of American organisational culture. His contacts in America and his adaptability to Western ways of thinking have opened up both American and Japanese markets and allowed him to gain information in the West more openly and at a faster rate than his Japanese competitors.

Genichi is beating his Japanese competitors and they are beginning to wonder why.

Kazuyo

Kazuyo's experience is different. A young graduate from the Nagoya University, she has spent a year engaged in English-language study and teaching in Australia. Compared to her male peers, she knows her prospects back in Japan are limited. Even though the government has recently introduced an equal employment opportunity law, she fears it will be a long time before the large companies change their policy of not employing young women graduates, or if they do, then sacking women when they marry. Her prospects lie in teaching or in a smaller business where women are given more opportunity.

She likes the freer life and opportunities offered to Australian women. Someday she hopes to be able to use the contacts she has made here in Australia to work here permanently.

Are these two people typical of younger Japanese or do they represent the signs of things to come?

A Clash of Cultures

We cannot assume that Genichi or Kazuyo are typical young Japanese but we can say that their experiences are a sign of changing times ahead for the Japanese. It is apparent that there is a growing number of younger Japanese people who want more individual independence than the Japanese culture currently allows. Some, like Genichi, are learning to have it both ways. Kazuyo believes that to have what she wants she may need to leave Japan.

Moreover, this new generation of Japanese represent a serious clash of cultures and a potential serious danger to Japanese economic predominance. This group wants more leisure, more job mobility, more space, more Western-style housing, more say, more individuality.

To what extent can the Japanese overcome these problems? How intransigent is the Japanese group culture to the more individualistic but reciprocal cultural behaviour we espouse and to which many younger Japanese currently aspire.

The Anatomy of Dependence

To answer this question, we need to look at what the Japanese say about themselves. In an insightful book on Japanese psychology entitled *The Anatomy of Dependence*, a Japanese psychiatrist, Takeo Doi, helps to explain why Japanese, and Australians and Americans find it so difficult to bridge the gap between the two cultures or to decide when yes might actually mean no in negotiation.

Generally speaking, Doi says, the Japanese like group action. It is extremely difficult for a Japanese to transcend the group and act independently. The reasons would seem to be that a Japanese person feels vaguely that it is treacherous to act on his or her own without considering the group to which he or she belongs, and feels ashamed even at doing something on his or her own.

Of course, group action is not unknown in the West nor is there anything intrinsically bad about strong group dependency. It is the capacity to be able to move from one group to the other or to act at times independently of it that is important, and that freedom is what individual Japanese presently lack. There is another important point that Takeo Doi believes distinguishes Japanese behaviour from Western behaviour.

Not only, he says, has Japan failed to establish the freedom of the individual as distinct from the group, but there is, it seems, a serious dearth of the type of public spirit that transcends both individual and group. This too would seem to have its origins in the fact that the Japanese divide their lives into inner and outer sectors, each with its own, different standards of behaviour, and no-one feeling the slightest oddity in this discrepancy.

It is this lack of a consistent set of universal or higher-order values that confuses Western societies when dealing with Japan. They tend to take certain values, like truthfulness and honesty, for granted as abstract concepts that will be consistently applied from one situation to another.

Networkers looking to link up with strong issues networks in Japan might encounter considerable difficulty as a result of these differences. As the nuclear family becomes the norm in Japan and other social supports decline, there is a strong need for a universal concern for youth for the aged, for women and for other issues. The lack of cross-group affiliation makes that very difficult at present to achieve, since the Japanese judge every situation in relation to the circle in which it occurs and find it hard to make links on an issues basis.

This might be the explanation of why feminism or unionism as a movement or other issues, for that matter, have not taken strong root in Japan. The vertical integration within organisations precludes such movements from developing a large following.

As Charles Y. Yang points out in a special report in the *Harvard Business Review* in December 1984:

> *A Sony engineer is a Sony employee first and last. He is vertically related to the members of his company rather than horizontally related to similar professionals in different organisations.*
>
> *The concept of vertical relationships also supports lifetime employment and may inhibit the formation of unions on a horizontal basis across different companies!*

Loyalty to the company would also preclude loyalty to an unrelated ideal. The only unifying ideal in the past, according to Doi, has been loyalty to the Emperor and this child–parent dependency also pervades other group relationships. It is described by the word amae, for which there is no precise equivalent translation in the English language.

Takeo Doi's book on Japanese dependency concludes, in general terms, that "freedom of the individual" does not mean that the individual is free in himself, or herself, as he or she is; (a peculiarly western concept) freedom is only acquired through the fact of participation in another group originally unrelated to the group to which he or she belongs. In effect he or she is free to become locked into another group, but is not able to move to a strategic positioning between numerous groups (the "crossroads" situation).

But this is the essence of networking success. Jumping from one pond to another and sometimes larger ponds, and not necessarily staying in any ponds for long but being able to access them all, is what personal networking for success is about. This kind of individual freedom is not available to the Japanese because their culture prevents them from moving out from their primary group on which they are totally dependent, a locked-in but often comfortable situation. If they do move out, however, they have to develop total allegiance to the new group.

What of the Future – Japan?

George Simmel in his book *Conflict and Group Affiliations* suggests that in the West the potential to move from one group to another is a relatively modern phenomenon. It did not exist in mediaeval times. Hence the inevitably tragic consequences of the love affairs of Romeo and Juliet and Tristan and Isolde who dared to defy the group norm. It could be that the Japanese are now beginning to go through a similar process of social transition hundreds of years after the West has forgotten that its own social structure once locked people into tight-knit groups, from which there was no escape.

John Naisbitt, in *Re-inventing the Corporation* is optimistic about the Japanese capacity to open their doors and their thinking to people of different cultures. But this seems to be simplistic.

Charles Y. Yang takes a different perspective, pointing out that Japanese organisations are running into considerable difficulties in the face of the information economy because of the restrictions their culture imposes on cross-group movement and, therefore, the quick and efficient transfer of information and group action. He indicates that the Japanese are fully aware of their present dilemmas. One indication of increased mobility is the advent of executive search consultancies – a relatively new phenomenon in Japan.

Ohmae in *The Mind of the Strategists* describes how he introduced the notion of the samurai (the individual warrior invested with a particular task) into corporations as a culturally sympathetic way of getting fast and decisive action within the slow consensus Japanese system.

A recent article in the *Sydney Morning Herald*'s *Good Weekend* titled "Theory F The One Ingredient that Makes Japanese Management Work: Fear" by Joel Kotkin and Yoriko Kishimoto, indicates, as Genichi and Kazuyo also illustrate, that among Japanese workers themselves there is a growing disillusionment with group loyalty and dependency and an attraction to the Western philosophy of individual freedom. How widespread this is, is difficult to judge but it is doubtful whether Japanese women, who are every bit as well educated as Japanese men, will remain content with the positions assigned them, particularly those who have spent any period in the West.

The point is that these changes in Japanese society mean that the locked-in/small-pond quality of life, which characterises that society, is likely to break down. It is likely to be replaced by more open personal networks and, therefore, more opportunities to be entrepreneurial. It is likely that there will be more opportunities to innovate, rather than being so much a nation of close-knit, group-minded, very clever copiers and adapters of innovations originated elsewhere.

Japan can be freed up more, to utilise more fully the human potentials of vast numbers of people in innovative and pond-jumping and pond accessible ways. The average man and woman will be more free to plug into alternative perspectives and really network to individual advantage and to find better solutions beyond the invisible barriers.

Those invisible barriers, the norms of traditional and especially group ways of doing things that have been handed down over many centuries, will gradually break down – and most probably in an accelerating fashion as more innovative, entrepreneurial pond-jumping and pond-assessing occurs. For this is the way of networking, one of the fundamentals, that new opportunities opened up are likely to snowball and open up still further opportunities, and so on.

When the Japanese have gone through a period of undoubted great difficulties and considerable trauma in cultural adjustment, they will come up the other side better equipped, we believe, to cope with the third wave and the new information economy. To use Naisbitt's term, they are even now caught up in a series of "megatrends", and the changing patterns of personal networking by the myriad of individuals will clearly be an underlying factor in the larger scale trends and more obvious signs of change. There will still be ponds everywhere, but they will be a little more permeable and changing in composition, with more mobility because of increased pond jumping and pond accessibility.

What of the Future – the United States?

In the meantime the most socially mobile society on earth, the United States, characterised by more open styles of networking and high levels of individually oriented entrepreneurship, will probably have to adapt styles by closing ranks a little more. To become more close-knit in personal networking styles, to work hard at making quality ponds and making them committed and more seepage proof, to prevent the leakage of ideas across the Northern Pacific to you-know-where. The reason is that once they get over there, the ideas are then likely to be systematically and fully enriched through the small-pond processes we described earlier in this chapter, that are so excellent in providing high levels of precision and commitment – the requisites of not just copying but copying with high level, value-added enhancement.

So the United States, in particular, will need to be more close-knit and more supportive in networking style and probably a little slower in decision-making processes – closer to what we termed earlier "big fish in small pond" status. The following aims should be kept in mind: concentrating on security of information and intellectual property; plus thoroughness, precision, commitment and all those other group processes popularly identified as belonging to Japanese management.

How America lost its dominance in the car industry is described historically in a book called *The Reckoning* by David Halverstain. The single most important factor in this decline was the closed arrogance of the moguls in the American car industry from Henry Ford down. Barbara Tuchman's book *The March of Folly* contains other similar lessons about American international relations. These chronicle the same cross-cultural prejudices and mistakes repeated again and again.

The richest nation on earth might find it hard to be less arrogant, less status-conscious, less individualistic, permeable and careful of its resources, including its human resources. Just as the second richest nation, Japan, might find it difficult to come to grips with its new changes. But in order to win so that everyone wins, some deep thinking has to go on around these culturally determined values. Australia and all other countries should be considering the very same questions. What are your national networking capabilities?

It is now in the interests of the Japanese to want to work closely and cooperatively with America and, indeed, all Western nations. They have run out of space and resources and their people are restless. They need other places to go and other fields to conquer. Significantly their growing affluence is their greatest danger.

While the Japanese go through this incredibly difficult and no doubt relatively long period of adjustment, American companies that do get their act together in the ways described above are likely to have a competitive edge over their

Japanese counterparts amidst the latter's social confusion as part of the fundamental readjustment processes. But in addition to the above factors, American companies will have to go through other cultural adaptations to make the most of the opportunities that will be presented to them by the coming confusion in Japanese society.

One of the major problems in the United States in the past has been the very isolation of the individual. The balance between the freedom of the individual to be a competitive, creative entrepreneur and to surround that person and the ensuing processes of product development with supportive structures, has to be struck and struck quickly. Authority and responsibility need to be transferred down the line.

Much of western management is in crisis simply because, as Lester Thurow says, in a recent lecture given at the American Academy of Science we are locked into a number of assumptions about how to do things. We reward the manager who builds his or her organisation and makes it grow heavy with people. Status is tied to the number of people supervised. If you don't have a secretary, this is seen as a loss of status. Senior executives like to appear very busy rather than accessible. Their secretaries can keep up that facade.

These are all culturally based attitudes and behaviours and they need to be examined for what they are. Technology can do a lot of the work a secretary once did. It can record messages, find a person wherever he or she is, store and retrieve information quickly, and it can be an aid to networking. What it can't do is provide those very important human skills that are the essence of successful networking in the information society – trust and reciprocity, an ever-widening circle of contacts and an open-minded perception.

The great Japanese strength in the past has centred on taking the best of inventions and ideas right from under the noses of the nations that invent them. This applies across the spectrum from the best in the automotive industry and the silicone chip to the theory of organisation. William Demming's quality circles (those now famous group product and management processes which, it is popularly believed, are the secret of Japanese success) came from America. They were rejected by managers in the United States then sold to and adapted by the Japanese to their own enormous economic advantage. In Professor Kumou's terms, closer international cooperation might well solve one of the most pressing Japanese problems. But on whose terms and at whose expense? It might be significant that the Japanese, not Americans, are publicly fostering this idea.

The experience to date is that it is not "win/win" with the Japanese in business. Not because they are dishonest or tough, but because the Western way of doing business is vulnerable and naive when it comes to understanding Japanese culture and how that translates into business negotiation. Westerners have got to take more responsibility for part of that current scenario. The current trade war between Japan and other countries, particularly America, indicates a growing awakening to that fact a determination to fight back and do business differently. Japan may well find that to survive, reciprocity and some 'universal' values like trust and honesty become part of its language of the future.

The central point in all cultures, be they Japanese, American, Australian or French and irrespective of what is happening within them, networks are increasingly important. This is because the power of information is becoming all persuasive and we are increasingly more deeply entrenched in an information-intensive society. In addition, through the internationalisation and deregulation of trade on goods and services and of capital movements involving international direct and portfolio investments, transactions in offshore money and capital markets, etcetera, the various national economies have become progressively more inter-dependent. The important issue is not whose culture and cultural manifestation would ultimately emerge triumphant. Networks are becoming even more important within all cultures and in their interrelationships with one another. There is, therefore, no choice about networks.

Interdependence means learning to understand each other, to do business in a way that leaves the other feeling they have not been "ripped off", and thereby to live happier and more complete lives.

Checklist

Chapter 14

- Important social changes are taking place in Japan which will have long term outcomes for the WORLD economy and for demand by Japanese young people for more personal freedom.
- This will have important ramifications for Japanese society and for a demand for open networking skills among Japanese people.
- Nevertheless, Japanese group dependency is likely to be the prevailing social value in Japan for many years to come and it is this essential difference which Western networkers must understand if they are to build networks in Japan.
- In order to do effective business with the Japanese the United States needs to come closer to them in terms of group cohesiveness, more supportive of individuals, and less careless with ideas.
- Arrogance, status consciousness, a mind closed to cultural differences are all obstacles in the path of attaining these objectives.
- Because all economies are now more closely linked with each other than at any previous time, anything that a nation does will affect their trading and non-trading partners.
- In the information era, we live in a network universe built upon interdependency. There is no choice about the importance of networks.

Chapter 15

You Can Do It

Get Going Now

Opportunities abound and they can often have a snowball effect, the more of them you discover the more of them you discover. But opportunities are often hard won – it is a matter of making the effort and networking your way across from certain ponds and into others and finding the opportunities. Of all your opportunities in life and business, nothing is achieved without effort. From your effort invested in reading this book, you will now agree that no effort is of value unless properly underpinned by the right sort of network. Your network.

From the starting point you have now, you should go and build the right networks, strengthen your existing networks, or simply understand your networks better. Start new networks, or prune and combine old networks. Unless you are particularly unusual, there will be room for improvement, things that you can do.

You can most fully unlock your potential for a better life by working on the networks closest to you, that is your personal networks. These comprise all your contacts plus the connections that those people have. These can open up for you incredible opportunities perhaps far from where you are physically, but not far from where you are right now in network terms; it simply requires a phonecall or two and the establishing of a few relationships in one direction or another.

We urge you, good friend... *go networking! unlock your potential and discover new opportunities now!*

Get out your personal telephone list, then enter various names and explore the opportunities on the next page (Figure 15.1).

Then you'll be going places.

CIVILIZATION INCORPORATED
I wonder if that crazy fool had any success networking?

Social Contacts

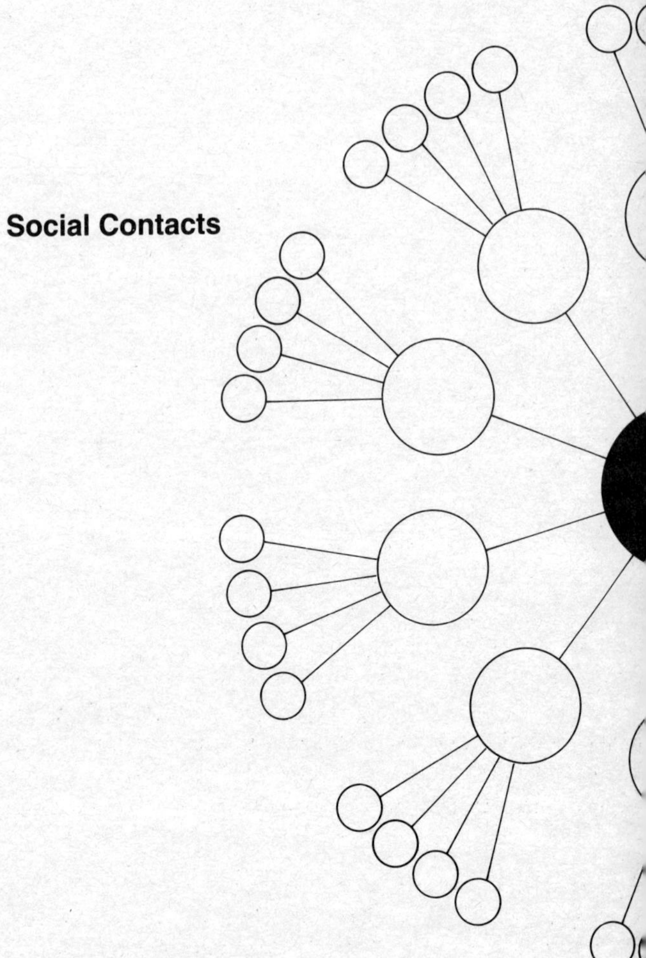

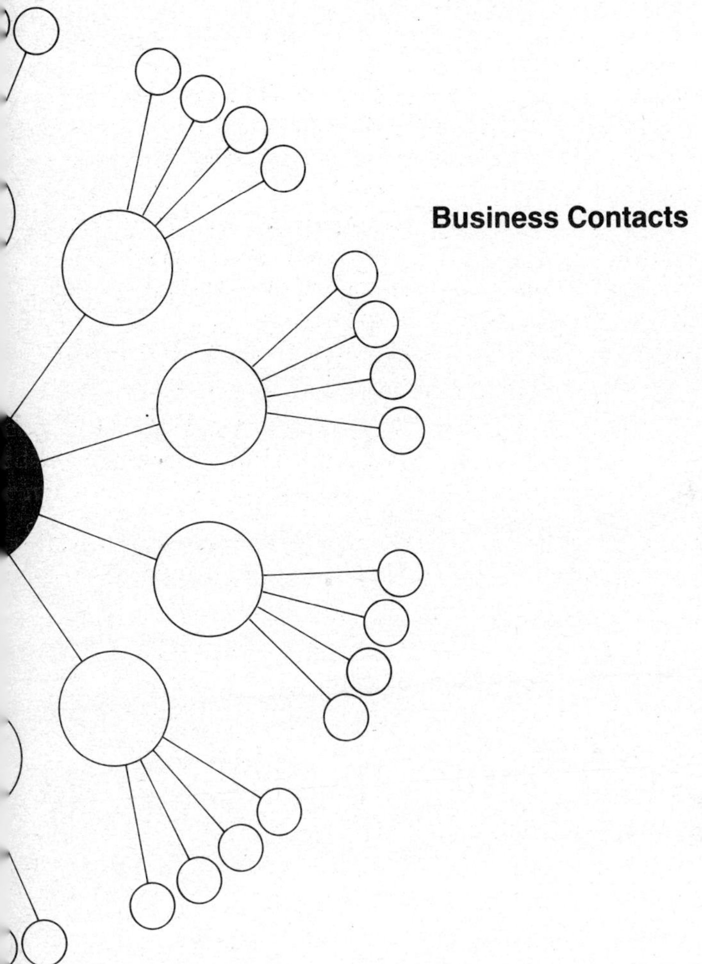

Figure 15.1
Your social and business contacts – your personal network

THE END

Bibliography

ANTHONY, WILLIAM. *Managing Your Boss.* New York, AMACOM, 1983.

BERGER, PETER L. AND LUCKMANN, THOMAS. *The Social Construction of Reality: a treatise in the sociology of knowledge*. Harmondsworth, England, Penguin, 1966.

BERGLAND, RICHARD. *The Fabric of the Mind*. Ringwood, Vic., Penguin, 1985.

BERNE, ERIC. *Games People Play: the psychology of human relationships*. London, Deutsch, 1964.

BERNE, ERIC. *What Do You Say After You Say Hello?* New York, Grove Press, 1972.

BLANCHARD, KENNETH AND JOHNSON, SPENCER. *The One Minute Manager*. New York, Morrow, 1982.

DE BONO, EDWARD. *Tactics: the art and science of success*. London, Collins, 1985.

BOTT, ELIZABETH. *Family and Social Network: roles, norms and external relationships in ordinary urban families*. London, Tavistock Publications, 1957.

CARNEGIE, DALE. *How to Win Friends and Influence People*. New York, Simon and Schuster, 1936.

CHANDLER, ALFRED. *Strategy and Structure: chapters in the history of the industrial enterprise.* Cambridge, Mass., Massachusetts Institute of Technology Press, 1962.

DEAL, TERRENCE E. AND KENNEDY, ALLAN A. *Corporate Cultures: the rites and rituals of corporate life*. Reading, Mass., Addison-Wesley, 1982.

DEMMING, WILLIAM E. *Quality, Productivity and Competitive Position*. Cambridge, Mass., Massachusetts Institute of Technology, Center for Advance Engineering Study, 1982.

DOI, TAKEO. *The Anatomy of Dependence: the key analysis of Japanese behaviour*. Translated by John Bester. Tokyo, Kodansha International Ltd., 1981.

FERGUSON, MARILYN. *The Acquarian Conspiracy: personal and social Transformation in the 1980's*. London, Routledge and Kegan Paul, 1981.

GORDON, THOMAS. *Leader Effectiveness Training, L.E.T: the no-lose way to release the productive potential of people*. New York, Wyden Books, 1977.

GORDON, THOMAS. *P.E.T., Parent Effectiveness Training: the tested new way to raise responsible children*. New York, New American Library, 1975.

GORDON, THOMAS AND BURCH, NOEL. *T.E.T., Teacher Effectiveness Training,* New York, David McKay, 1977.

GUMPERT, DAVID AND BOYD, DAVID " The Loneliness of the small business owner". *Harvard Business Review*, vol. 62, no. 6, November/December, 1984, pp. 18-24.

HALVERSTAM, DAVID. *The Reckoning*. London, Bloomsbury, 1987.

HARRIS, THOMAS. *I'm O.K, You're O.K* London, Pan Books, 1973.

HEALD, TIM. *Networks: who we know and how we use them*. London, Hodder and Stoughton, 1983.

HILMER, FREDERICK G. *When The Luck Runs Out: the future for Australians at work*. Sydney, Harper and Row, 1985.

HOFSTEDE, GEERT. *Cultures Consequences*. Beverly Hills, California, Sage, 1980.

KANTER, ROSABETH MOSS. *The Change Masters: corporate entrepreneurs at work*. London, Allen and Unwin, 1984.

KOTKIN, JAL AND KISHIMOTO, YORIKO. *Theory F. "The One Ingredient that Makes Japanese Management Work: Fear"*. Good Weekend Magazine, Sydney Morning, Herald. May 9-10, 1986.

KOTTER, JOHN. *The General Managers*. New York, Free Press, 1982.

KUMON, SHUMPEI. "The Knowledge Game: the impact of information on social systems." *Speaking of Japan*, vol. 5, no. 46, October 1984, pp. 6-9.

LEVERING, ROBERT, MOSKOWITZ, MILTON AND KATZ, MICHAEL. *The Hundred Best Companies to Work for in America*. Reading, Mass., Addison-Wesley, 1984.

MALTZ, MAXWELL. *Psychocybernetics: a new way to get more out of life*. Englewood Cliffs, N.J., Prentice-Hall, 1960.

MILGRAM, STANLEY. "The Small-World Problem". *Psychology Today*, vol. 1, no. 1, May 1967, pp. 60-67.

NAISBITT, JOHN. *Megatrends: ten new directions transforming out lives*. New York, Warner Books, 1982.

NAISBITT, JOHN AND ABURDENE, PATRICIA. *Re-inventing the Corporation: transforming your job and your company for the new information society*. London, MacDonald, 1986.

OHMAE, KENICHI. *The Mind of the Strategist: the art of Japanese business*. New York, McGraw-Hill, 1982.

PEALE, NORMAN VINCENT. *The Power of Positive Thinking*. Kingswood, Surrey, World's Work, 1953.

PETERS, THOMAS J. AND WATERMAN, ROBERT H. *In Search of Excellence: lessons from America's best run companies*. New York, Harper and Row, 1982.

PINCHOT, GIFFORD III. *Intrapreneuring*. New York, Harper and Row, 1985.

RIES, IVOR. "How Australia fails in Japan." *Business Review Weekly*, vol. 8, no. 16, April 25, 1986, pp. 31-32.

RINGER, ROBERT. *Winning Through Intimidation*. Greenwich, Conneticut, Fawcett Publications, 1973.

SIMMEL, GEORG. *Conflict and Group Affiliation*. Glencoe Ill., Free Press, 1955.

THUROW, LESTER C. "Management in Crisis". Lecture given at the American Academy of Science, Australian Broadcasting Commission, June 1986.

TOFFLER, ALVIN. *The Third Wave*. New York, Morrow, 1980.

TUCHMAN, BARBARA W. *The March of Folly: from Troy to Vietnam*. London, Michael Joseph, 1984.

WELCH, MARY SCOTT. *Networking: the great new way for women to get ahead*. New York, Harcourt, Brace, Jovanovich, 1980.

YANG CHARLES. "Demystifying Japanese management pracitces". *Harvard Business Review*, vol. 62 no. 6, November/December, 1984, pp. 172-182.